I·N·S·O·L·V·E·N·C·Y

# Disqualification and Personal Liability of Directors

**Third Edition**

**L. S. Sealy MA LLM PhD**
*Barrister and Solicitor of the High Court of New Zealand, Fellow of Gonville and Caius College and Lecturer in the University of Cambridge*

CCH Editions Limited
TAX, BUSINESS AND LAW PUBLISHERS

Published by CCH Editions Limited
Telford Road, Bicester, Oxfordshire OX6 0XD
Tel. (0869) 253300, Facsimile (0869) 245814.
DX: 40162 Bicester

| | |
|---|---|
| USA | Commerce Clearing House Inc., Chicago, Illinois. |
| CANADA | CCH Canadian Limited, Toronto, Ontario. |
| AUSTRALIA | CCH Australia Limited, North Ryde, NSW. |
| NEW ZEALAND | Commerce Clearing House (NZ), Auckland. |



**Legislation reproduced**

The publisher advises that the legislation in this publication is not the authorised official version. In its preparation, however, the greatest care has been taken to ensure exact conformity with the law as enacted.

While copyright in all the legislation resides in the Crown, copyright in indexes and annotations relating to that legislation is vested in the publisher.

**British Library Cataloguing in Publication Data**
Sealy, L. S. (Leonard Sedgwick, *1930–*
Disqualification and personal liability of directors.
– 3rd. ed. – (Insolvency)
1. Great Britain. Companies. Insolvency. Liability of directors. Law
I. Title II. Series
344.106′78

First published 1986
Second edition 1987
Third edition 1989

ISBN 0 86325 199 4



Typeset and printed in the United Kingdom by The Eastern Press Limited, Reading.

# Preface

The insolvency legislation of 1985 and 1986 introduced a new code of conduct for company directors. It sets standards of competence, diligence and skill which are far more demanding than under the previous law. Breaches may lead to disqualification orders, which prohibit the director from holding any office in a company or taking part in its management for up to 15 years, and to compensation orders which impose on him personal liability to contribute to an insolvent company's assets.

Both during the passage of the Insolvency Bill through Parliament and in statements made since, the Government has expressed its determination to make use of these sanctions far more vigorously than in the past, and there has already been a significant increase in the number of disqualification and compensation orders made against directors under the new insolvency regime.

These reforms took effect on 28 April 1986, when the relevant parts of the Insolvency Act 1985 were brought into force. Further extensive alterations to the law were made by the two consolidating statutes of 1986, the Insolvency Act 1986 and the Company Directors Disqualification Act 1986. These Acts came into operation together on 29 December 1986.

The third edition of this book brings the text fully up to date and takes account of all the legislative changes referred to above. The work has also been expanded to include an examination of the provisions of the Companies Act 1985 under which directors may be made personally liable for their company's debts.

In the text which follows, the abbreviations listed below are used.

| | |
|---|---|
| CA 1985 | Companies Act 1985 |
| CDDA 1986 | Company Directors Disqualification Act 1986 |
| Cork Report | *Report of the Review Committee on Insolvency Law and Practice* (Cmnd 8558, 1982) |
| IA 1985 | Insolvency Act 1985 |
| IA 1986 | Insolvency Act 1986 |

Extracts from the Insolvency Act 1986 and the Company Directors Disqualification Act 1986 are reproduced in Appendix I.

*L. S. Sealy*, February 1989

# About the Publisher

CCH Editions Limited is part of a world-wide group of companies that specialises in tax, business and law publishing. The group produces a wide range of books and reporting services for the accounting, business and legal professions. The Oxfordshire premises are the centre of all UK and European operations.

All CCH publications are designed to provide practical, authoritative reference works and useful guides, and are written by CCH's highly qualified and experienced editorial team and specialist outside authors.

CCH Editions Limited publishes bound books and loose-leaf reporting services for the United Kingdom and other European countries, as well as distributing the publications of its overseas affiliate companies.

# Acknowledgement

The official forms set out in Appendix IV of this book are Crown Copyright and are reproduced with the kind permission of the Controller of Her Majesty's Stationery Office.

# Contents


| | | Page |
|---|---|---|
| Preface | | v |
| About the Publisher | | vi |
| **1** | **Introduction: The Insolvency Legislation of 1985 and 1986** | 1 |
| ¶101 | The legislation on director disqualification and compensation orders | 1 |
| ¶102 | The Insolvency Act 1985 | 1 |
| ¶103 | Background to the Insolvency Act 1985: the Cork Report | 2 |
| ¶104 | The White Paper of 1984 | 2 |
| ¶105 | The Insolvency Bill | 2 |
| ¶106 | The consolidating Acts of 1986 | 2 |
| ¶107 | The consolidating Acts: application and commencement | 3 |
| ¶108 | Extension to bodies other than companies | 4 |
| ¶109 | Liability of 'shadow directors' and others | 4 |
| ¶110 | Extension to directors of building societies | 5 |
| ¶111 | Extension to former members of an insolvent partnership | 6 |
| **2** | **Director Disqualification: Nature and Effect of Orders: Procedure** | 7 |
| ¶201 | Nature and effect | 7 |
| ¶202 | Duration of order | 8 |
| ¶203 | Leave of court to act notwithstanding order | 9 |
| ¶204 | Who may apply? | 10 |
| ¶205 | Administration and enforcement | 10 |
| ¶206 | Procedure | 10 |
| ¶207 | Register of disqualification orders | 11 |
| ¶208 | Disqualification orders not to be cumulative | 11 |
| ¶209 | Analogous ban on undischarged bankrupt | 11 |
| ¶210 | Variation of disqualification orders | 12 |
| **3** | **Director Disqualification: The Background** | 13 |
| ¶301 | Disqualification of directors under the Companies Acts | 13 |
| ¶302 | Changes made by the Insolvency Act 1985 | 14 |

| | Page |
|---|---|
| ¶303 Consolidation of the law | 14 |
| ¶304 Further amendment: the Financial Services Act 1986 | 15 |
| **4 Director Disqualification: Grounds** | 16 |
| ¶401 Grounds for making a disqualification order | 16 |
| SECTION 2: DISQUALIFICATION ON CONVICTION OF AN INDICTABLE OFFENCE | 16 |
| ¶402 Conviction of an indictable offence | 16 |
| SECTION 3: DISQUALIFICATION FOR PERSISTENT BREACHES OF COMPANIES LEGISLATION | 17 |
| ¶403 Persistent breaches of companies legislation | 17 |
| SECTION 4: DISQUALIFICATION FOR FRAUD, FRAUDULENT TRADING OR BREACH OF DUTY REVEALED IN A WINDING-UP | 18 |
| ¶404 Fraud, etc. in a winding-up | 18 |
| SECTION 5: DISQUALIFICATION ON SUMMARY CONVICTION | 20 |
| ¶405 Summary conviction under companies legislation | 20 |
| SECTION 6: DISQUALIFICATION OF UNFIT DIRECTORS OF INSOLVENT COMPANIES | 20 |
| ¶406 Replacement of Companies Act 1985, s. 300 | 20 |
| ¶407 Company must have 'become insolvent' | 21 |
| ¶408 Liquidator to report on directors' conduct | 22 |
| ¶409 Time-limit of two years | 22 |
| ¶410 Meaning of 'unfitness' | 22 |
| ¶411 Comments on Sch. 1 | 24 |
| ¶412 Judicial decisions on the concept of unfitness | 25 |
| ¶413 Relevance of conduct in relation to other companies | 27 |
| ¶414 Implications of the new definition of unfitness | 27 |
| ¶415 Shadow directors | 28 |
| ¶416 Duration of order | 28 |
| SECTION 8: DISQUALIFICATION AFTER INVESTIGATION OF COMPANY | 29 |
| ¶417 Statutory powers of investigation | 29 |
| ¶418 Disqualification of director after investigation | 29 |
| ¶419 Comment on s. 8 | 30 |
| SECTION 10: DISQUALIFICATION ON GROUNDS OF FRAUDULENT OR WRONGFUL TRADING | 30 |
| ¶420 Fraudulent and wrongful trading | 30 |

| | | Page |
|---|---|---|
| **5** | **Directors' Personal Liability: Fraudulent Trading** | 32 |
| ¶501 | Fraudulent trading | 32 |
| ¶502 | Recommendations of the Cork Committee | 32 |
| ¶503 | Wrongful trading: the new law | 33 |
| ¶504 | Law on fraudulent trading to continue | 33 |
| ¶505 | Remedies and procedure | 33 |
| ¶506 | Disqualification for participation in fraudulent trading | 34 |
| ¶507 | Application to insolvent partnerships | 34 |
| **6** | **Directors' Personal Liability: 'Wrongful Trading'** | 35 |
| ¶601 | The concept of wrongful trading | 35 |
| ¶602 | Marginal note irrelevant | 36 |
| ¶603 | The statutory definition | 36 |
| ¶604 | The meaning of 'gone into insolvent liquidation' | 37 |
| ¶605 | 'A person who is or has been a director' | 37 |
| ¶606 | 'At some time before the commencement of the winding-up | 38 |
| ¶607 | 'Knew or ought to have concluded' | 38 |
| ¶608 | Director exonerated if he 'took every step with a view to minimising potential loss' | 39 |
| ¶609 | Implications of the new law | 40 |
| ¶610 | Practical consequences for directors | 41 |
| ¶611 | Procedure | 42 |
| ¶612 | Application of payments | 42 |
| ¶613 | Disqualification on grounds of wrongful trading | 42 |
| ¶614 | No anticipatory declarations | 42 |
| ¶615 | The first judicial ruling on wrongful trading | 42 |
| **7** | **Directors' Personal Liability: Acting While Disqualified: Use of Prohibited Company Name** | 43 |
| ¶701 | Personal liability for breach of disqualification order | 43 |
| ¶702 | Who is liable? | 43 |
| ¶703 | Re-use of prohibited company name | 44 |
| ¶704 | Extension to directors of building societies | 45 |
| ¶705 | Applications for leave to use a prohibited name | 45 |
| **8** | **Directors' Personal Liability Under the Companies Act 1985** | 47 |
| ¶801 | Introduction | 47 |
| ¶802 | Liability upon cheques, etc. on which company's name is wrongly stated | 47 |

| | Page |
|---|---|
| ¶803 Liability where public company commences business prematurely | 48 |
| ¶804 Directors' personal liability where shares are purchased or redeemed out of capital | 48 |
| **9 Applications for Leave to Act as a Director During a Disqualification Order** | 49 |
| ¶901 Statutory provisions | 49 |
| ¶902 Time and mode of application | 50 |
| ¶903 Court to which application is made | 50 |
| ¶904 Procedure | 50 |
| ¶905 Conditions | 50 |
| **10 Insolvency Practitioners and Their Role** | 52 |
| ¶1001 Requirement that insolvency practitioners should be qualified | 52 |
| ¶1002 Duty of insolvency practitioner to report on conduct of directors of insolvent company | 52 |
| **11 Transitional Provisions** | 54 |
| ¶1101 The new legislation: commencement dates | 54 |
| ¶1102 Transitional provisions: events before 28 April 1986 | 54 |
| ¶1103 Transitional provisions: director disqualification | 55 |
| ¶1104 Transitional provisions: offences and default orders before 1 June 1977 | 55 |
| ¶1105 Other transitional provisions | 55 |
| **Appendix I: Text of Relevant Statutory Provisions** | 57 |
| **Appendix II: Explanation of Statutory Terms** | 79 |
| **Appendix III: Reported Cases** | 81 |
| **Appendix IV: Forms** | 91 |
| **Case Table** | 99 |
| **Legislation Finding List** | 101 |
| **Index** | 105 |

## ¶107 The consolidating Acts: application and commencement

All the parts of the Insolvency Act 1986 which are discussed in this book, and the whole of the Company Directors Disqualification Act 1986, extend to Scotland, but not to Northern Ireland (IA 1986, ss. 440, 441; CDDA 1986, s. 24).

Sections 1–5, 11, 13–14 and 16–18 of the Company Directors Disqualification Act 1986 and s. 213 of the Insolvency Act 1986 are consolidations of provisions of the Companies Act 1985, which have all been in force in their present or an equivalent form for many years. Sections 12–16, 18 and Sch. 2 of the Insolvency Act 1985 (now replaced by the Company Directors Disqualification Act 1986, ss. 6–10, 15 and Sch. 1) came into effect on 28 April 1986. The remaining provisions falling within the present study became operative with the implementation of the two 1986 statutes on 29 December 1986.

New subordinate legislation was enacted to supplement these statutory reforms, and where necessary this has since been amended or replaced to follow developments in the relevant Acts.

The rules and regulations in question, with their commencement dates, are as follows:

- the Insolvent Companies (Reports on Conduct of Directors) Rules 1986 (SI 1986 No. 611), effective 28 April 1986 (now superseded by SI 1986 No. 2134, below);
- the Insolvent Companies (Disqualification of Unfit Directors) Proceedings Rules 1986 (SI 1986 No. 612), effective 28 April 1986 (now superseded by SI 1987 No. 2023, below);
- the Insolvent Companies (Reports on Conduct of Directors) (Scotland) Rules 1986 (SI 1986 No. 626 (S. 59)), effective 28 April 1986 (now superseded by SI 1986 No. 1916, below);
- the Insolvent Companies (Reports on Conduct of Directors) (No. 2) (Scotland) Rules 1986 (SI 1986 No. 1916 (S. 140)), effective 29 December 1986;
- the Companies (Disqualification Orders) Regulations 1986 (SI 1986 No. 2067), effective 29 December 1986;
- the Insolvent Companies (Reports on Conduct of Directors) No. 2 Rules 1986 (SI 1986 No. 2134), effective 29 December 1986;
- the Insolvent Partnerships Order 1986 (SI 1986 No. 2142), effective 29 December 1986;
- Act of Sederunt (Company Directors Disqualification) 1986 (SI 1986 No. 2296 (S. 168)), effective 29 December 1986;
- the Insolvent Companies (Disqualification of Unfit Directors) Proceedings Rules 1987 (SI 1987 No. 2023), effective 11 January 1988.

In general, the new law does not have retrospective application, so as to apply, for example, to an insolvency which began after the relevant commencement date. For the transitional provisions, see Chapter 8 below.

## ¶108 Extension to bodies other than companies

The sections of the Insolvency Act 1986 relating to director disqualification apply not only to companies registered under the Companies Acts but to a wider range of organisations.

For the purposes of the Company Directors Disqualification Act 1986, s. 11, which makes it an offence for an undischarged bankrupt to act as a director or take part in the management of a company (see ¶209), the term 'company' includes an unregistered company, a building society and a company incorporated outside Great Britain which has an established place of business in Great Britain (CDDA 1986, s. 22(2)). For practical purposes, an 'unregistered company' here means a company incorporated by private Act of Parliament, other than a railway company (IA 1986, s. 220(1)).

For the purpose of construing all the other provisions of the Company Directors Disqualification Act 1986 except s. 11, the expression 'company' includes any company which may be wound up under Pt. V of the Insolvency Act 1986 (a formula which embraces, *inter alia*, unregistered companies, overseas companies and insolvent partnerships) and any building society (CDDA 1986, s. 22(2)).

## ¶109 Liability of 'shadow directors' and others

Many of the statutory provisions discussed in this book apply not only to the directors of a company but also to its 'shadow directors'. This expression is defined in the Company Directors Disqualification Act 1986, s. 22(5) and the Companies Act 1985, s. 741(2) to mean a person in accordance with whose directions or instructions the directors of a company are accustomed to act (excluding a person who gives advice in a professional capacity). It obviously covers the case where a puppet board is set up which acts on the dictates of a non-director who masterminds the company's activities from behind the scene. However, it could also apply to a holding company which exercises a degree of control over decision making by the board of its subsidiary. A bank, also, could be caught within the definition if it had given 'directions or instructions' (as distinct from *professional* advice) to a client company at a time when insolvency was threatening: *Re a Company No. 005009 of 1987* (1988) 4 BCC 424 (see ¶605 below).

In addition, the scope of some sections extends to former directors and former shadow directors (e.g. IA 1986, s. 214 (wrongful trading)); while others are concerned with persons who are 'knowingly parties to the carrying on of the business' of a company (e.g. IA 1986, s. 213 (fraudulent trading)), or 'involved in the management' of a company (e.g. IA 1986, s. 217 (re-use of prohibited company name)). The wording of the particular provision must in each case be referred to in order to establish whether anyone else is affected, over and above the directors of the company.

Judicial decisions have clarified doubts regarding the scope of the Company Directors Disqualification Act 1986 in two respects. Although these cases were decided under the previous legislation, there is no doubt that they would be regarded as offering authoritative guidance to the construction of the 1986 Act also.

In *Re Lo-Line Electric Motors Ltd & Ors* [1988] Ch. 477; (1988) 4 BCC 415, Browne-Wilkinson V.-C. held that the court's power to make a disqualification order extended to a *de facto* director. The respondent in that case had resigned as director from one of the companies concerned but had in fact returned after an interval and run the company until it ceased trading, and in regard to three other companies had acted as a director without ever being formally appointed.

In *Re Eurostem Maritime Ltd & Ors* [1987] PCC 190, the court expressed the view, *obiter*, that it had power to disqualify a director in respect of a foreign company that was being wound up in England, and it held that in proceedings against the director of an English company his conduct in relation to foreign companies of which he was also a director could be taken into consideration.

## ¶110 Extension to directors of building societies

Parts of the legislation discussed in this book have been made applicable to the directors of building societies by s. 120 and Sch. 18, para. 17(3) of the Building Societies Act 1986. This amendment, which was made with reference to the Insolvency Act 1985, was not incorporated into the consolidating legislation of 1986, but is reproduced at the appropriate place in the extracts of the 1986 legislation set out in Appendix I (see CDDA 1986, s. 7). These amendments became operative on 1 January 1987.

The parts of the Acts which apply to the directors of building societies are the Company Directors Disqualification Act 1986, ss. 6–10 (disqualification of directors for unfitness and wrongful trading) and the Insolvency Act 1986, ss. 212 and 214–217 (summary remedy against delinquent directors, personal liability for wrongful trading, restriction on re-use of company names). A reference to a 'company' is deemed by the amending legislation to include a reference to a building society.

It is expressly provided that the concept of 'shadow director' is not to be extended to building societies. Note also that although the director of a building society may be liable for wrongful trading, there is no corresponding liability for fraudulent trading under the Insolvency Act 1986, s. 213.

## ¶111 Extension to former members of an insolvent partnership

Section 420 of the Insolvency Act 1986, taken in conjunction with the Company Directors Disqualification Act 1986, s. 21(2), allows provisions of the insolvency and director disqualification legislation to be extended to apply to situations where an insolvent partnership is being wound up. This has been done by the Insolvent Partnerships Order 1986 (SI 1986 No. 2142), operative from 29 December 1986. The effect of this subordinate legislation is to treat an insolvent partnership as if it were an unregistered company, so that it may be wound up under the Insolvency Act 1986, Pt. V, and to deem the members of an insolvent partnership which is being wound up in this way to be 'directors' of that 'company'. The provisions of IA 1986 relating to wrongful trading, etc. will therefore be applicable to the members of insolvent partnerships in the same way as if they had been directors of a company that is being wound up insolvent. In addition, ss. 6–10, 15, 19(*c*) and 20 of the Company Directors Disqualification Act 1986 and Sch. 1 to that Act are also made to apply to the members of insolvent partnerships – i.e. those provisions relating to disqualification for 'unfitness' and participation in wrongful or fraudulent trading. This extension of the disqualification law is in principle anomalous, for the justification for the imposition of a director disqualification order is invariably stated to be that the delinquent director has abused the privilege of limited liability – a privilege which is not enjoyed by the members of a partnership.

# 2 Director Disqualification: Nature and Effect of Orders: Procedure

## ¶201 Nature and effect

A disqualification order prohibits the person named, without the leave of the court, from:

- being a director of a company;
- being a liquidator or administrator of a company;
- being a receiver or manager of a company's property;
- in any way, either directly or indirectly, being concerned or taking part in the promotion, formation or management of a company (CDDA 1986, s. 1(1)).

'Management' for this purpose includes both the internal and external affairs of a company: *R* v *Austen* (1985) 1 BCC 99,528 (a case concerning the fraudulent raising of finance). In *R* v *Campbell* [1984] BCLC 83 a management consultant who acted as adviser to the board of a company was held to have 'been concerned in' and 'taken part in' its management; but this case may be contrasted with the Australian decision *Re Magna Alloys and Research Pty Ltd & Ors* (unreported, 19 September 1975: see CCH *British Company Law and Practice*, ¶29-650), where a former director who confined his activities strictly to advisory work was held not to have breached the equivalent section of the New South Wales Act. In a recent Australian case, *CCA* v *Bracht* (1989) 7 ACLC 40, the court considered that the concept of 'management' required an involvement of some kind in the decision-making process of the company. Here B, a banned person, had negotiated credit facilities on behalf of the company and had entered into negotiations with its landlord concerning a rent increase, but it was claimed that another person who was a director had the final say in all financial decisions made on behalf of the company and signed all the cheques. The court ruled that 'management' requires activities involving some responsibility but not necessarily of an ultimate kind:

negotiating terms with bankers, etc. could be sufficient, even though those terms had to be confirmed. Advice given to management, participation in decision-making processes and execution of management's decisions going beyond the mere carrying out of directions is sufficient.

A disqualification order may be made against a company or other corporate body, since the Act uses the word 'person' rather than 'individual'. This is confirmed by the Company Directors Disqualification Act 1986, s. 14.

Differing views have been expressed regarding the nature and purpose of a disqualification order. On the one hand, it may be seen in the nature of a punishment for misconduct – a view which is reinforced by the fact that the courts have, on occasion, revised or lifted a disqualification order when a director has appealed against a criminal sentence (see, e.g. *R* v *Green and Green* (1981) 3 Cr App R (S) 22; *R* v *Russen & Ors* (unreported, 6 July 1984, cited by Dr Janet Dine, (1988) 9 Co. Law 213, at p. 215). On the other hand, it may be seen as a measure taken for the protection of the public, as appears from the extracts cited from the cases in Appendix III, below. The latter view seems to have gained ground in the more recent cases; but this may in part be due to the fact that these have mostly dealt with disqualification orders imposed on the ground of 'unfitness', while the earlier decisions were concerned with directors who had been convicted of criminal misconduct. This whole question and its implications are discussed by Dr Dine in the article referred to above.

It is a criminal offence punishable by up to two years' imprisonment and/or a fine to contravene a disqualification order (CDDA 1986, s. 13), and the offender may also be declared to be personally liable for all the debts that are incurred: see ¶701 below.

Where a body corporate is guilty of an offence of acting in contravention of a disqualification order, and it is proved that a director, manager, secretary or similar officer was implicated in the contravention, that officer is liable to be held guilty of the offence and punished personally, in addition to the body corporate itself (CDDA 1986, s. 14(1)). Where the affairs of a body corporate are managed by its members (e.g. in the case of a Scottish firm), a member is similarly liable to be punished (s. 14(2)).

## ¶202 Duration of order

The maximum length and (for CDDA 1986, s. 6) the minimum length of a disqualification order is specified separately in each of the sections which define the grounds on which an order may be made (CDDA 1986, ss. 2–10). The court may fix any duration within the limits stated, and, except in the case of s. 6 (which is expressed in mandatory terms), it may also decide that it is not appropriate to make any order. The decided cases show that a 'tariff' has been developed, under which the period fixed by the court is made proportionate to the seriousness of the offence, with the maximum set by the Act being reserved for defaults of the most serious nature. Examples from the reports include *R* v *Austen* (1985) 1 BCC 99,528 (in which a pattern of dishonest conduct involving some £300,000 led to disqualification for ten years); *Re Lo-Line Electric Motors Ltd & Ors* [1988] Ch. 477; (1988) 4 BCC 415 (wrongful trading, misuse of Crown debts: three years); *Re Civica Investments Ltd & Ors* [1983] BCLC 456 (extensive default in filing obligations, not wilful or deliberate, followed by remedial action: one year); *Re Arctic Engineering Ltd & Ors* [1986] 1 WLR 686; (1985) 1 BCC 99,563 (liquidator and receiver defaulting over 35 returns: caution but no disqualification because of repercussions on staff and clients, and because non-compliance was not wilful).

The penalties imposed in a number of unreported cases have been listed in an article by Dr Janet Dine (see (1988) 9 Co. Law 213, at p. 216). These include *Re Blacklager Ltd* (ChD, 26 February 1987): a 'reckless disregard' for the financial position of the company – six years; *Re VAB Plating Ltd* (ChD, 11 April 1986): the director had 'consciously and deliberately been living at the expense of his creditors' – eight years; *Re BBK Interiors Ltd* (ChD, 2 June 1987): 'a deliberate course of conduct guaranteed to cause the maximum loss to the Government and maximum damage to the good image of business generally and to the office of company director' – 13 years.

In *R* v *Foster* (4 July 1972, unreported) it was held that the period of disqualification must run from the date of the order itself and cannot be post-dated so as, for example, to commence at the end of a custodial sentence. In practice, orders are declared to become 'effective' 21 days after the date of the order, unless the court orders otherwise: see the Insolvent Companies (Disqualification of Unfit Directors) Proceedings Rules 1987 (SI 1987 No. 2023, r. 9).

## ¶203 Leave of court to act notwithstanding order

The court may, either at the time when a disqualification order is made against a person or subsequently, grant him leave to act as a director or in some other capacity during the currency of the order. For example, in *Re Lo-Line Electric Motors Ltd & Ors* [1988] Ch. 477; (1988) 4 BCC 415, a disqualified person was allowed to continue to act as a director of two named family companies, subject to certain safeguards.

An undischarged bankrupt, who by virtue of the Company Directors Disqualification Act 1986, s. 11 is subject to an automatic statutory ban on acting as a director, etc., may similarly be granted leave to act by the court.

The procedure to be followed in regard to an application for leave, and the considerations which the court is likely to take into account in deciding whether to grant leave, are discussed in Chapter 9.

## ¶204 Who may apply?

An application for a disqualification order on any grounds set out in the Company Directors Disqualification Act 1986, ss. 2–5 may be made by the Secretary of State or the Official Receiver, or by the liquidator or any past or present member or creditor of any of the companies concerned (CDDA 1986, s. 16(2)). Under ss. 6 and 8, only the Secretary of State or (if the Secretary of State so directs) the official receiver is competent to apply (s. 16(2)). The jurisdiction in the case of s. 10 (participation in wrongful or fraudulent trading) may be invoked 'whether or not an application for such an order is made by any person' (s. 10(1)). It would appear from this wording that anyone interested in the litigation may ask the court for an order: in the normal case the liquidator or other applicant under the Insolvency Act 1986, ss. 213 or 214 would be the most appropriate person. The court may also act under s. 10 of its own motion.

## ¶205 Administration and enforcement

The Department of Trade and Industry has established a Director Disqualification Unit to administer the new regime.

The statistics show that the number of disqualification orders made since the coming into force of the relevant provisions of the Insolvency Act 1985 has increased significantly, and is continuing to rise.

In the year ended 31 December 1988, a total of 332 orders were made – more than double the number recorded in the previous year.

## ¶206 Procedure

Section 16 of the Company Directors Disqualification Act 1986 describes the procedure to be followed in making application for a disqualification order. Not less than ten days' notice must be given to the person concerned, where the application is made to a court of civil jurisdiction. The appropriate court for an application can be determined only by reference to the particular section of the Act which is being relied on: see Appendix I for the text of the relevant provisions of the Act. This section will apply in all cases except: (a) where a disqualification order is made under the Company Directors Disqualification Act 1986, ss. 2 or 5, by the court which has convicted him of the relevant criminal offence, and (b) where disqualification is sought on the grounds of 'unfitness', for which special Rules have been made. These Rules are currently the Insolvent Companies (Disqualification of Unfit Directors) Proceedings Rules 1987 (SI 1987 No. 2023).

These Rules apply to applications made by the Secretary of State or the official receiver on the grounds of 'unfitness', including unfitness found following an investigation made by inspectors appointed by the Secretary of

State (CDDA 1986, ss. 6–8). Application is made in the High Court by originating summons and in the county court by originating application, supported by affidavit evidence. The respondent has 28 days after service of the proceedings to file his own affidavit evidence in reply. The case may be determined by a registrar or, in more serious or complex instances, adjourned for hearing by a judge. An order may be made in the absence of the respondent if he fails to appear.

## ¶207 Register of disqualification orders

The Registrar of Companies maintains a register of disqualification orders which is open to public inspection (CDDA 1986, s. 18). The register is maintained at the Companies Registration Offices in Cardiff, London and Edinburgh. No fee is payable for an inspection of the register. It is the duty of a designated officer of the court to notify the Secretary of State within 14 days of the making of any disqualification order, or of a grant of leave, or of any action taken by a court in consequence of which a disqualification order is varied or ceases to be in force (see the Companies (Disqualification Orders) Regulations 1986 (SI 1986 No. 2067)).

## ¶208 Disqualification orders not to be cumulative

The legislation contains an express provision that where a person is subject to more than one disqualification order, the periods are to run concurrently (CDDA 1986, s. 1(3)).

## ¶209 Analogous ban on undischarged bankrupt

In addition to the above provisions, the Company Directors Disqualification Act 1986, s. 11 prohibits an undischarged bankrupt from acting as director or liquidator of a company or directly or indirectly taking part in the promotion, formation or management of a company, except with leave of the court. This is a re-enactment of the provision formerly contained in the Companies Act 1985, s. 302.

The ban imposed upon an undischarged bankrupt is analogous in many ways to a director disqualification order, except of course that it applies automatically, without the need for a court order. In particular, in deciding whether leave should be granted to take part in management during the currency of the statutory prohibition (see Chapter 9), the court is likely to take similar considerations into account.

A similar prohibition may be imposed when a court which is administering the estate of an insolvent individual under Pt. VI of the County Courts Act 1984 revokes the order for administration (CDDA 1986, s. 12). Note that the 'administration order' referred to here relates to an individual debtor and has no connection with an administration order made in respect of an insolvent company under the Insolvency Act 1986, s. 8.

## ¶210 Variation of disqualification orders

No specific provision is made by the Company Directors Disqualification Act 1986 for the variation of a disqualification order, but this is something which the court can undoubtedly do in its inherent jurisdiction. That this is so is confirmed by the Insolvent Companies (Disqualification of Unfit Directors) Rules 1987 (SI 1987, No. 2023), r. 8(2), which declares that a disqualification order made in the absence of the respondent may be set aside or varied by the court on such terms as it thinks just. The Regulations (see ¶207 above) direct the appropriate officer of the court to notify the Secretary of State of any variation made in the terms of a disqualification order.

# 3 Director Disqualification: The Background

## ¶301 Disqualification of directors under the Companies Acts

The concept of director disqualification is not new. The Companies Act 1985, itself a consolidating Act, established in ss. 295–302 and Sch. 12 the legal framework for making and registering such orders, which is now continued by the Company Directors Disqualification Act 1986, and set out the grounds on which a disqualification order could be made under the law then in force. This list of grounds was modified and extended by ss. 12–16 of the Insolvency Act 1985 so as to include all the cases discussed in Chapter 4 below. In outline, the heads under which a disqualification order could be made under the former law were:

(1) *Conviction of an indictable offence in connection with company management, etc.* (CA 1985, s. 296; now CDDA 1986, s. 2): see ¶402 below.

(2) *Persistent default in filing obligations under the Companies Act* (CA 1985, s. 297; now CDDA 1986, s. 3): see ¶403 below.

(3) *Fraudulent trading, fraud or breach of duty revealed in a winding-up* (CA 1985, s. 298; now CDDA 1986, s. 4): see ¶404 below.

(4) *Being a director of two companies successively wound up insolvent within five years, and found 'unfit'* (CA 1985, s. 300). This head of disqualification has not survived the reforms of 1985 and 1986: see ¶406 below.

(5) *Summary conviction for offence under the Companies Act, together with other convictions or defaults* (CA 1985, s. 299; now CDDA 1986, s. 5): see ¶405 below.

Cases decided under the former legislation may throw some light on the interpretation of the provisions of the Company Directors Disqualification Act 1986, but they should be treated with caution: they may well be poor guides to the likely judicial approach under the new Act. For example, in *Re Churchill Hotel (Plymouth) Ltd & Ors* [1988] 4 BCC 112, the court found the respondent unfit to be a director but, exercising its discretion under the

Companies Act 1985, s. 300 (now repealed), declined to make a disqualification order against him. There is no similar discretion under the Company Directors Disqualification Act 1986, s. 6: if unfitness is found, the court must now impose a mandatory disqualification for at least two years.

## ¶302 Changes made by the Insolvency Act 1985

The following are the principal changes which were made by the insolvency legislation of 1985–86 in relation to director disqualification:

(1) Section 300 of the Companies Act 1985 has been *repealed*, so that it is no longer necessary for a director to be associated with *two* successive insolvencies before he can be disqualified for unfitness; instead, *one* insolvency will now suffice (IA 1985, s. 12; now CDDA 1986, s. 8: see ¶406 below).

(2) Two *additional grounds* for making a disqualification order have been introduced, namely:

   (i) 'unfitness' found following an investigation of a company's affairs on the order of the Secretary of State for Trade and Industry (IA 1985, s. 13; now CDDA 1986, s. 8: see ¶417 below); and

   (ii) being held responsible as a director for a company's 'wrongful' or 'fraudulent' trading (IA 1985, s. 16; now CDDA 1986, s. 10: see ¶420 below).

(3) In addition to the existing criminal penalties, a person who contravenes a disqualification order can now be made *personally liable* to contribute to the assets of the company concerned, and similar sanctions are imposed on anyone who knowingly acts on the instructions of a disqualified person (IA 1985, s. 18; now CDDA 1986, s. 15: see Chapter 7 below).

(4) The rule was introduced that disqualification orders should run concurrently and not cumulatively (IA 1985, Sch. 6, para. 1(3), amending CA 1985, s. 295(2)).

(5) Liquidators, administrative receivers and other 'office-holders' are now required to make a return to the Secretary of State in regard to every insolvent company, reporting on the conduct of all its directors and shadow directors so that the Secretary of State can, if he thinks fit, institute proceedings seeking a disqualification order: see below, Chapter 10.

## ¶303 Consolidation of the law

When the legislation relating to insolvency was consolidated in 1986, the Company Directors Disqualification Act 1986 was enacted to bring together into one consolidated Act all the provisions of the Companies Act 1985 and the Insolvency Act 1985 relating to director disqualification.

## ¶304 Further amendment: the Financial Services Act 1986

Section 198(2) of the Financial Services Act 1986 has amended s. 8 of the Company Directors Disqualification Act 1986 by adding references to the reports of Department of Trade and Industry Inspectors made under the provisions of ss. 94 and 177 of the Financial Services Act 1986 and to information or documents obtained under s. 105 of that Act: see ¶418 below.

There was a further amendment made by the Criminal Justice (Scotland) Act 1987 (see ¶418 below).

# 4 Director Disqualification: Grounds

## ¶401 Grounds for making a disqualification order

The grounds on which a disqualification order may be made are set out in ss. 2–10 of the Company Directors Disqualification Act 1986. The discussion follows the same sequence as the statute.

## SECTION 2: DISQUALIFICATION ON CONVICTION OF AN INDICTABLE OFFENCE

## ¶402 Conviction of an indictable offence

The court may make a disqualification order against a person where he is convicted of an indictable offence (e.g. fraud) in connection with the promotion, formation, management or liquidation of a company or with the receivership or management of a company's property (CDDA 1986, s. 2; formerly CA 1985, s. 296). Although the offence in question must be one which is *capable* of being prosecuted on indictment, it is not necessary for the purposes of s. 2 that the actual conviction should have been obtained on indictment. Nor does the section make it a prerequisite that the company should be insolvent or in liquidation.

The decided cases show that the scope of s. 2 is not limited to offences which arise out of the management of the internal affairs of the company: it may extend to offences in relation to third parties. For instance, in *R* v *Corbin* ((1984) 6 Cr App R (S) 17) the offender had been party to fraudulent transactions entered into by the company in its dealings with certain finance companies, and in *R* v *Appleyard* ((1985) 81 Cr App R 319) the company's managing director had set fire to one of its buildings in an attempt to defraud its insurers. It is not necessary that there should be any actual misconduct of the company's affairs, whether internal or external: in *R* v *Georgiou* (1988) 4 BCC 322, a disqualification order was made against a person who had carried on an unauthorised insurance business through the medium of a limited company, and had been convicted on indictment of an offence under the Insurance Companies Act 1982.

If the offence is dealt with by a court of summary jurisdiction (e.g. a magistrates' court), the maximum disqualification period is five years; otherwise, it is 15 years. There is no prescribed minimum period.

For the meaning of 'the court' and 'indictable offence' in relation to this section, reference should be made to the text of the Act (see Appendix I).

## SECTION 3: DISQUALIFICATION FOR PERSISTENT BREACHES OF COMPANIES LEGISLATION

### ¶403 Persistent breaches of companies legislation

The court may make a disqualification order up to a maximum of five years against a person who has been persistently in default in his duty of making returns or delivering accounts and other documents to the Registrar of Companies under the Companies Acts and the Insolvency Act 1986 (CDDA 1986, s. 3, replacing CA 1985, s. 297). For this purpose, there is a presumption that a person has been 'persistently in default' if he has been convicted of a default, or has been required by court order to make good a default, three times in the preceeding five years (s. 3(2), (3)), but this does not preclude proof in other ways (s. 3(2)).

In *Re Arctic Engineering Ltd* [1986] 1 WLR 686; (1985) 1 BCC 99,563 it was held that the term 'persistently' requires some degree of continuance or repetition. A person may persist in the same default, or persistently commit a series of defaults. However, it is not necessary to show that a person has been culpable, in the sense of evincing a deliberate disregard of the statutory requirements, although such culpability can be taken into account in considering whether to make a disqualification order and, if so, for how long. In the case in question, the respondent was an insolvency practitioner employing a staff of 30 who at any one time had about 600 liquidations and receiverships on his hands. There had been default in making some 35 returns within the statutory five-year period. He pleaded that he had not intended to flout the law, and that the defaults were due to administrative oversight or human error: they represented a very small percentage of the total returns which his office had been required to make in the relevant period. The court nevertheless held that he had been 'persistently in default' and, whilst declining to make a disqualification order in the special circumstances of the case, warned that an order might well be made in a similar case in the future.

The obligation to file documents with the registrar of companies and to make returns is most often placed by the Companies Acts upon the company itself rather than any particular officer or officers, but some duties (e.g. to deliver annual accounts) are specifically imposed upon the directors, and other duties directly upon a liquidator, administrative receiver or similar office-holder. However, even where the duty lies with the company, it is often provided that the company and any 'officer in default' shall be guilty of an offence. An 'officer in default' is 'any officer of the company who knowingly and wilfully authorises or permits the default . . . or contravention' (CA 1985, s. 730(5)). A director can thus be guilty of an offence when it is his company which is primarily in breach of the Act. However, for the Company Directors Disqualification Act 1986, s. 3 to apply, it is the director himself who must have been convicted, and not merely the company. In the same way, a default order, to be relevant, must be one made against the director concerned and not his company.

There is a close connection between this section and s. 5 (¶405 below), which is also concerned with persistent breaches of company law, defined in a similar way. However, the court which has jurisdiction to make an order under s. 3 is 'any court having jurisdiction to wind up' any of the relevant companies, while s. 5 contemplates that the order will be made by the court of summary jurisdiction which has actually convicted the director, or by another magistrates' court in the same area: see ss. 3(4), 5(2).

## SECTION 4: DISQUALIFICATION FOR FRAUD, FRAUDULENT TRADING OR BREACH OF DUTY REVEALED IN A WINDING-UP

### ¶404 Fraud, etc. in a winding-up

The court which has jurisdiction to wind up a company may make a disqualification order against a person if it appears in the winding-up of the company that he has been guilty of fraudulent trading (whether he has been convicted or not), or has otherwise been guilty, while an officer or liquidator of the company or receiver or manager of its property, of any fraud or breach of duty in relation to the company (CDDA 1986, s. 4, continuing CA 1985, s. 298).

It is not necessary for the purposes of s. 4 that the company should be insolvent. The maximum period of disqualification is 15 years.

On the meaning of 'fraudulent trading', see Chapter 5 below. It is curious that s. 4 still retains the requirement that the fraudulent trading should 'appear in the course of the winding up' of the company, when the criminal offence of fraudulent trading (CA 1985, s. 458) no longer has any link with winding-up.

There is some overlap between this section and s. 2, but whereas a conviction is necessary for s. 2 but not s. 4, the latter applies only if there is a winding-up.

A disqualification order based on fraudulent trading may be made under s. 10 of the Company Directors Disqualification Act 1986, as well as under this section; but for s. 10 to apply an order must first have been made declaring the person liable to contribute to the company's assets under s. 213 of the Insolvency Act 1986.

In applying this section (or its equivalent) in the past, the courts have always insisted upon the strict standard of proof appropriate to criminal charges. It is likely that less use will be made of s. 4 in future, at least in those cases where no conviction is sought (and a consequential disqualification order under s. 2): the burden of proof is much lighter under both s. 6 (unfitness) and s. 10 (wrongful trading), and either of these sections will be an appropriate alternative in most cases.

To be liable to disqualification under s. 4(1)(*b*), the person concerned must have been involved as a director (or shadow director: see s. 4(2)) of the company or have held one of the other offices listed. (The section refers to an 'officer or liquidator of the company or receiver or manager of its property'. For the meaning of the term 'officer', see Appendix II.) The following appear to be among those caught by the section:

- A director
- A shadow director (s. 4(2))
- A secretary (CA 1985, s. 744)
- A 'manager' (for the meaning of this term, see Appendix II)
- A liquidator
- A receiver (including a receiver and manager and an administrative receiver).

Those less certainly included (depending on the construction of the term 'officers') are:

- An auditor
- The supervisor of a voluntary arrangement (made under IA 1986, ss. 1–7)
- An administrator (appointed under IA 1986, s. 8).

In contrast, fraudulent trading under s. 4(1)(*a*) may be committed by any person who was knowingly a party to the carrying on of the fraudulent business – potentially a much wider class of defendant.

## SECTION 5: DISQUALIFICATION ON SUMMARY CONVICTION

### ¶405 Summary conviction under companies legislation

Section 5, like s. 3, authorises the making of a disqualification order against a person who has been guilty of failing to make returns, etc. to the Registrar of Companies on at least three occasions within a period of five years. The main difference is that s. 3 requires a separate application to be made to a court of civil jurisdiction for an order after one or more convictions have been recorded by another court, while under s. 5 the disqualification order is made by a court of summary jurisdiction, normally on the same occasion as the latest conviction of the offender.

As with s. 3, a 'default order' (see s. 3(3)(*b*) and ¶403 above) is treated as equivalent to a conviction for the purposes of reckoning up the three 'defaults' required by s. 5; but there has to be an actual conviction on the occasion when the disqualification order is made. The three or more 'defaults' may, however, consist of several convictions recorded at the same hearing (s. 5(3)).

The maximum period of disqualification under s. 5 is five years.

## SECTION 6: DISQUALIFICATION OF UNFIT DIRECTORS OF INSOLVENT COMPANIES

### ¶406 Replacement of Companies Act 1985, s. 300

The Cork Committee (*Report*, para. 1818) recommended that s. 300 of the Companies Act 1985 (see ¶301 above) should be tightened up in a number of respects, and this was done by repealing the section and substituting a new provision (now CDDA 1986, s. 6). The changes which have been made include:

- an order can be made against a director who has been associated with only *one* insolvent liquidation;
- where unfitness is found, and the other requirements of the section are satisfied, disqualification is *mandatory* rather than discretionary;

- the court must impose disqualification for a *minimum* period of *two years*.

There was a further recommendation of the Cork Committee which was not adopted: this would have allowed an application to the court for a disqualification order to be made directly by the liquidator, and sometimes even by a creditor. Section 6, however, provides that only the Secretary of State (or the official receiver, if directed to do so by the Secretary of State) may initiate proceedings. An aggrieved creditor is expected to make his complaint to the insolvency practitioner concerned and rely on him to report the matter to the Secretary of State, or perhaps to make it directly to the Secretary of State.

## ¶407 Company must have 'become insolvent'

Before the jurisdiction of s. 6 can be invoked, the company must have 'become insolvent'; but this expression has an artificial meaning for the purposes of s. 6 which will not necessarily mean that the company is insolvent in a business sense. Under s. 6(2), a company will 'become insolvent' if:

(a) it goes into liquidation at a time when its assets are insufficient to pay its debts, liabilities and winding-up expenses; or

(b) an 'administration order' is made (irrespective of the solvency or otherwise of the company at any relevant time); or

(c) an 'administrative receiver' is appointed (again, irrespective of the company's actual financial state).

'Administration order' and 'administrative receiver' are new terms introduced by the insolvency legislation of 1985 and 1986: the former refers to a novel procedure devised as an alternative to liquidation, and the latter is a receiver or manager appointed to enforce a general floating charge (see further, Appendix II). In either of these cases, a director may have a disqualification order made against him although it turns out that the company is not in reality insolvent. Conversely, even when a company *has* 'become insolvent' in a business sense, the section will not necessarily apply – there must also have been one of the events (a), (b) or (c) listed above.

The expression 'has become insolvent' in the sense defined by s. 6(2) is relevant also for the purposes of Sch. 1, which sets out guidelines for the test of directors' 'unfitness': see ¶410 below.

In the discussion which follows, it will be assumed that the insolvent company is in liquidation and that the insolvency practitioner who is responsible as the 'office-holder' (see s. 7(3)) is the liquidator; but the provisions of the Act will apply in a similar way to situations where the company is in the hands of an administrator or an administrative receiver.

## ¶408 Liquidator to report on directors' conduct

The first step towards securing a disqualification order under s. 6 is taken by the liquidator (or other 'office-holder'), who must report any case of suspected unfitness to the Secretary of State (see s. 7(3)). For this purpose he is to have regard to the person's conduct as a director of the company which has become insolvent, but he may also take into account the director's conduct in relation to any other company. Former directors are included within the section. The Secretary of State may then apply to the court for an order, or direct the official receiver to do so. The 'office-holders' of the company (i.e. a liquidator, administrator or administrative receiver), and any former 'office-holders', have a duty under s. 7(4) to co-operate with inquiries, by furnishing information and producing such of the company's books and records as may reasonably be required.

Regulations made under the Act require all 'office-holders' of insolvent companies to make returns to the Secretary of State, using prescribed forms. In these returns, the insolvency practitioner concerned must give a report on every director, former director and shadow director of the company, and state whether he considers that the conduct of each such person makes him unfit to be concerned in the management of a company: see below, Chapter 10.

## ¶409 Time-limit of two years

The application must be made within two years from the day when the company 'became insolvent' (i.e. went into liquidation, administratorship or receivership); but the court may, exceptionally, give leave to make a later application (s. 7(2)). No guidance is given as to the grounds upon which the court may grant such an extension of time.

## ¶410 Meaning of 'unfitness'

Under the Companies Act 1985, s. 300 (which has now been repealed), the question whether a person was 'unfit' to be concerned in the management of a company was a matter for the court to determine in its own judgement. However, the Company Directors Disqualification Act 1986, in s. 9, contains statutory directions to which the court is required to have regard in particular in assessing the question of unfitness.

The statutory criteria are set out in Sch. 1 in two Parts. Part I applies in all cases, and Pt. II applies in addition to Pt. I where the company in question has 'become insolvent' (as that phrase is defined in s. 6(2)). Where the application is made under s. 6, it will always be the case that the company in respect of which application is made has 'become insolvent', so that both

Parts of the Schedule will be relevant. If the director's conduct in relation to other companies is brought into the reckoning under s. 6(1)(*b*), it will be necessary for the court to determine whether any of those companies has (or had) 'become insolvent' in order to see whether Pt. II applies; and this inquiry will always be necessary in an application under s. 8.

The criteria set out in Sch. 1 may be summarised as follows:

*Part I – Matters applicable in all cases*

(1) Any misfeasance or breach of a fiduciary or other duty owed by the director to the company.

(2) Any misapplication of assets or conduct making him accountable to the company.

(3) His part in any improper transfer of assets intended to defraud creditors (IA 1986, s. 423).

(4) His part in any failure by the company to keep proper records and registers and to file annual returns, etc.

(5) His part in any failure to prepare annual accounts and directors' and auditors' reports.

*Part II – Matters applicable where company has become insolvent*

(6) His part in the causes of the company's insolvency.

(7) His part in the company's failure to supply goods and services which have been paid for in whole or in part.

(8) His part in any transaction which is 'at an undervalue' or which is voidable as a 'preference' (under IA 1986, ss. 238–240) or which is void (under IA 1986, s. 127) because made after the commencement of the winding-up (or under the corresponding provisions in Scots law).

(9) His part in any failure to summon a creditors' meeting in a creditors' voluntary winding-up (IA 1986, s. 98).

(10) His part in any failure to comply with various other procedural obligations imposed upon directors in an insolvency (e.g. preparing a statement of affairs).

## ¶411 Comments on Sch. 1

One or two items in the above list perhaps deserve some comment. Paragraph (7) in ¶410 reflects the general anxiety (especially in consumer circles) about the lack of protection given by the former law to members of the public who made payments to a company (e.g. for goods on mail-order) and lost everything, as mere unsecured creditors, if it went into liquidation. Attempts to give such pre-payments preferential treatment by law were defeated during the debates on the Insolvency Bill, but para. (7) was inserted instead, so that the courts can now use disqualification as a sanction against the irresponsible use of consumer-prepayments to boost a company's ailing cash-flow. It may sometimes be prudent therefore, when a company's financial stability is in any doubt, for directors to take steps to set up a separate account in which advance payments are held on the customers' behalf (see *Re Kayford Ltd* [1975] 1 WLR 279).

Paragraph (8) refers to certain new provisions first introduced by the Insolvency Act 1985, s. 101 and now contained in the Insolvency Act 1986, ss. 238–240. These replace the old concepts of 'fraudulent conveyance' (Law of Property Act 1925, s. 172) and 'fraudulent preference' (CA 1985, s. 615) with the new terms 'transaction at an undervalue' and 'preference'. Although the new definitions no longer have the implications of moral turpitude associated with the word 'fraudulent', the transactions in question are still liable to be set aside as improper, and by virtue of the present provision any director involved is liable to be declared 'unfit'.

Section 127 of the Insolvency Act 1986, like its predecessor (CA 1985, s. 522), avoids dispositions of property, etc. made by a company after the commencement of a winding-up unless authorised by the court. Although there will not necessarily be any impropriety on the part of a director in such a case, the Schedule makes it clear that if there is, it may be a matter indicative of 'unfitness'.

Paragraph (9) adds a further sanction to the Insolvency Act 1986, s. 98, which was enacted to outlaw the former practice known as 'centrebinding'. Under this abuse, directors delayed the appointment of a creditors' nominee as liquidator for a period long enough to allow corporate assets to be disposed of in a way which suited their own interests and defeated the creditors' rights.

It should be emphasised that the guidelines set out in Sch. 1 are not intended to be a definitive list of directors' obligations. The court's power to condemn any conduct as evidencing unfitness is unrestricted. Further, the items in the Schedule may be modified from time to time by regulations made by the Secretary of State (s. 9(4)).

## ¶412 Judicial decisions on the concept of unfitness

There is now a growing corpus of reported decisions on the question of 'unfitness'. Some of these cases were concerned with the interpretation of the concept for the purposes of the repealed Companies Act 1985, s. 300, which had no statutory schedule of 'guidelines', and so are only of indirect relevance to the construction of the term as it is used in the Company Directors Disqualification Act 1986, ss. 6 and 8. A summary of some of these reported cases appears in the present paragraph and, in tabular form, in

Appendix III, where extracts from some of the leading judgments are also included.

In *Re Bath Glass Ltd* (1988) 4 BCC 130, it was ruled that to reach a finding of unfitness the court should be satisfied that the director had been guilty of one or more serious failures, whether deliberately or through incompetence, to perform those duties which are attendant on the privilege of trading through companies with limited liability, and that any misconduct as a director could be relevant, even if it did not fall within a provision of the companies or insolvency legislation.

In *Re Lo-Line Electric Motors Ltd & Ors* [1988] Ch. 477, at p. 486; (1988) 4 BCC 415, at p. 419, Browne-Wilkinson V.-C. said: 'Ordinary commercial misjudgment is in itself not sufficient to justify disqualification. In the normal case, the conduct complained of must display a lack of commercial probity although I have no doubt that in an extreme case of gross negligence or total incompetence disqualification could be appropriate'.

A number of cases have focused upon one particular issue – the failure by a company and its directors to set aside sufficient funds to meet Crown debts for PAYE, NIC and VAT, in effect using this money as working capital as insolvency looms. In *Re Dawson Print Group Ltd & Anor* (1987) 3 BCC 322 (a case decided under the repealed Companies Act 1985, s. 300), Hoffmann J took the view that such conduct did not necessarily breach standards of commercial morality sufficiently to warrant the imposition of a disqualification order on the grounds of 'unfitness'; but most later cases have taken a different attitude on this point, whilst stressing that each case must be judged on its own facts. For example, in *Re Stanford Services Ltd & Ors* (1987) 3 BCC 326, Vinelott J emphasised that traders are obliged to maintain records of the Crown debts in question, so that the court can infer that a director in these circumstances is either in breach of his duty to keep himself adequately informed about the company's financial position or is acting improperly in allowing the company to trade using Crown moneys to aid its cash flow. Other cases in which the misuse of Crown debts was held to justify the making of a disqualification order include *Re Churchill Hotel (Plymouth) Ltd & Ors* (1988) 4 BCC 122, *Re Bath Glass Ltd* (above) and *Re Lo-Line Electric Motors Ltd* (above). In the last of these cases Browne-Wilkinson V.-C. said: 'I consider the use of moneys which should have been paid to the Crown to finance continuation of an insolvent company's business more culpable than the failure to pay commercial debts'.

Other features which the courts have frequently relied upon as justifying the making of a disqualification order include:

- failing to keep proper books of account;
- failing to file returns with the registrar of companies;

- continuing to trade when the director knew, or ought to have known, that the company was insolvent;
- drawing excessive remuneration;
- paying directors' salaries (effectively out of creditors' moneys) when the company was insolvent;
- failing to submit a statement of affairs;
- continuing to accept customer prepayments when in financial difficulties;
- diverting moneys from one company to another without proper regard for the separate interests of each company.

[Note: some of the matters listed above, which were taken into account by judges in cases brought under the Companies Act 1985, s. 300 and its predecessors, have now been given statutory force by the Insolvency Act 1986, Sch. 1.]

On the other hand, factors which have weighed with the court in deciding that a disqualification order should not be made, or that a reduced period of disqualification would be appropriate, have included:

- acting on professional advice;
- employing a qualified company secretary or finance director;
- absence of dishonesty;
- readiness to make a personal financial commitment to the company;
- capitalisation of accumulated profits so as to strengthen the company's equity base;
- reliance on regular budgets and forecasts (even though subsequently shown to have been inaccurate);
- the fact that outside factors not within the directors' control contributed to the company's misfortunes;
- evidence that other companies have been successfully and properly run by the respondent.

## ¶413 Relevance of conduct in relation to other companies

The court, in deciding whether a person's conduct makes him 'unfit to be concerned in the management of a company', will primarily be concerned with his conduct in relation to the insolvent company in which he has until recently held office. However, s. 6(1)(*b*) empowers the court to have regard also to his conduct as a director of 'any other company or companies'. For this purpose, it is not necessary that the other company or companies should also have 'become insolvent'; but it is only his conduct *as a director* of those companies that is relevant. For this purpose, 'director' includes 'shadow director': see s. 6(3). A *de facto* director would probably also be included: *Re Lo-Line Electric Motors Ltd & Ors* [1988] Ch. 477; (1988) 4 BCC 415: see ¶109.

It was held in *Re Bath Glass Ltd* (1988) 4 BCC 130 that the director's conduct in relation to other companies is to be looked at only 'for the purpose of finding additional matters of complaint': in other words, it is not open to the director to adduce evidence that his conduct in relation to other companies has been impeccable in an endeavour to show that a disqualification order would be inappropriate. However, it is clear from *Re Bath Glass Ltd* and other decided cases that the court will take account of the fact that a director has been associated with other, responsibly run, companies in fixing the length of a disqualification order and in giving leave to be involved in the management of a company during the currency of an order (see Chapter 8).

In *Re Eurostem Maritime Ltd & Ors* [1987] PCC 190, the court held that in proceedings against the director of an English company his conduct in relation to foreign companies of which he was also a director could be taken into consideration.

## ¶414 Implications of the new definition of unfitness

Much of what is set out in Sch. 1 is not novel: in part, it merely restates and serves to reinforce the former law – a persistent failure to file company returns, for instance, will bring a director within the scope of para. (4) in ¶410 above but would equally well have justified disqualification under the provision which is now consolidated as the Company Directors Disqualification Act 1986, s. 3: see ¶403 above. Read as a whole, these provisions do not impose new duties on directors or demand higher standards; rather, they make it possible to exact a salutary penalty for breaches of duty which previously were allowed to go unpunished because of inadequacies in the law enforcement process.

The conscientious director should have nothing to fear; but the fraudulent or reckless or irresponsible director is likely to find that the prosecuting authorities are now less inhibited and the law less indulgently disposed towards him. Even so, all directors will naturally look to the Schedule for guidance on proper standards of conduct. The wording of Sch. 1 appears to be directed primarily at those directors who have taken an active part in the company's affairs, rather than at those whose role has been nominal or who have involved themselves only intermittently; but there is no reason to suppose that even a non-executive director of a small family company should be immune from responsibility when those who are actively running the company allow accounts, records and returns to fall into disarray. In reality, however, the Secretary of State is most likely to concentrate his resources on those who have been culpably implicated in wrongdoing, and it will be the new 'wrongful trading' provisions (see Chapter 6 below) that the inactive director will have most cause to fear.

## ¶415 Shadow directors

Section 6 applies not only to directors and former directors, but also to 'shadow directors' (s. 6(3)). (On this term, see ¶109.) A *de facto* director who had acted as such without proper appointment has been held to be included within the scope of the precursor to s. 6: *Re Lo-Line Electric Motors Ltd & Ors* [1988] Ch. 477; (1988) 4 BCC 415 (a case on CA 1985, s. 300).

The former members of an insolvent partnership are treated as directors for the purposes of the present section (see ¶111 above); and its application was extended to include the directors of building societies, with effect from 1 January 1987 (see ¶110 above).

## ¶416 Duration of order

Section 6 is the only provision in the legislation which prescribes a minimum disqualification period (two years). In *Re Bath Glass Ltd* (1988) 4 BCC 130, at p. 133, Peter Gibson J expressed the view that the fact that the legislature had imposed this mandatory disqualification period was relevant to deciding whether a director should be classed as 'unfit': only conduct which was sufficiently serious to warrant such a period of disqualification would justify a conclusion that a person was 'unfit'. This was to be contrasted with other provisions of the Company Directors Disqualification Act 1986, such as s. 10 ('wrongful trading': see ¶420 below), which prescribed no minimum period. From this we may infer that wrongful trading for which disqualification for a six or twelve-month period might be appropriate would not be conduct justifying a finding of unfitness.

The maximum disqualification period under s. 6 is 15 years (s. 6(4)).

# SECTION 8: DISQUALIFICATION AFTER INVESTIGATION OF COMPANY

## ¶417 Statutory powers of investigation

The Secretary of State has power under the Companies Act 1985, ss. 431–441 to appoint inspectors to investigate the affairs of a company in a number of situations, e.g.:

- on the application of the company itself or a section of its members (s. 431);
- if the court so orders (s. 432(1));
- following a report of suspected criminal conduct made to him at the investigation of the liquidator in a voluntary winding up (IA 1986, s. 218(4), (5)); or
- of his own motion, if it appears to him that there are circumstances suggesting fraud or irregularity (s. 432(2)).

Under other provisions (CA 1985, ss. 447, 448), the Secretary of State has power to require production to him of books or papers relating to a company, and to ask for an explanation of them to be given.

The Financial Services Act 1986, by ss. 94, 177, extends these powers of investigation to include (a) the affairs of a unit trust scheme or a collective investment scheme, and (b) possible contraventions of the insider dealing legislation (Company Securities (Insider Dealing) Act 1985, ss. 1, 2, 4, 5). Under s. 105 of the Financial Services Act 1986 there is also the power to investigate the affairs of any person currently or formerly carrying on investment business or thought to be such a person.

## ¶418 Disqualification of director after investigation

Section 8 of the Company Directors Disqualification Act 1986 gives power to the court to make a disqualification order, on the application of the Secretary of State, if it appears from a report made to him or from information or documents obtained by him under the above provisions and other provisions (see below) that it is expedient in the public interest that an order should be made against a director or former director of any company. The court must also be satisfied that the conduct of this person in relation to the company makes him unfit to be concerned in the management of a company.

Section 8 was amended by the Financial Services Act 1986, s. 198(2) to include reports made to the Secretary of State under ss. 94 and 177 and information or documents obtained under s. 105 of that Act (see ¶417 above). These amendments operate from 15 November 1986 for the reference to ss. 94 and 177 (see SI 1986 No. 1940 (C. 69)) and from 18 December 1986 for the reference to s. 105 (see SI 1986 No. 2246 (C. 88)). A reference to s. 52 of the Criminal Justice (Scotland) Act 1987 was added by s. 55(*b*) of that Act, with effect from 1 January 1988 (see SI 1987 No. 2119 (C. 62 (S. 143)). These sections empower the Secretary of State to investigate certain matters, e.g. authorised unit trust schemes and insider dealing. A reference to s. 2 of the Criminal Justice Act 1987 was added by s. 145(*b*) of the Criminal Justice Act 1988 with effect from 12 October 1988 (see SI 1988 No. 1676

(C. 60)). It empowers the Director of the Serious Fraud Office to make certain investigations. The Companies Bill 1988, when enacted, will extend s. 8 even further, to include reports made following investigations ordered for the purpose of assisting an overseas regulatory authority: see cl. 71 of the Bill.

### ¶419 Comment on s. 8

The following points may be made in comparing s. 8 with s. 6:

- only the Secretary of State may make an application;
- the court's power is discretionary rather than mandatory;
- the term 'director' again includes a 'shadow director';
- there is no minimum period of disqualification, but the same maximum of 15 years;
- the person's conduct in relation to companies other than that which has been investigated is not to be taken into account;
- the test of 'unfitness' laid down by s. 9 and Sch. 1 of the Company Directors Disqualification Act 1986 is the same. Note that only Part I of the Schedule (headings (1)–(5) in ¶410 above) will be relevant if the company has not 'become insolvent'; for this purpose the phrase 'become insolvent' has the artificial meaning defined by s. 6(2) and discussed in ¶407 above.

## SECTION 10: DISQUALIFICATION ON GROUNDS OF FRAUDULENT OR WRONGFUL TRADING

### ¶420 Fraudulent and wrongful trading

The topics of fraudulent trading (IA 1986, s. 213) and wrongful trading (IA 1986, s. 214) are discussed in Chapters 5 and 6 below. These sections empower the court to declare that the persons responsible shall be liable to make such contributions to the company's assets as it thinks proper. Section 10 of the Company Directors Disqualification Act 1986 adds a further sanction by stating that, when a court makes such a declaration against a person, it may if it thinks fit also make a disqualification order against him. This it may do on the application of any person, or of its own motion without any special application being made. The section appears to assume that the disqualification order will be made in the same proceedings as the declaration of liability, but conceivably it might be the subject of a separate, later application.

Section 213 of the Insolvency Act 1986 (fraudulent trading) applies to 'any persons who were parties to the carrying on of the business'; and so in such a case s. 10 of the Company Directors Disqualification Act 1986 may extend to include someone who was not a director or shadow director. Only a director or shadow director, however, may be made liable under the wrongful trading section (IA 1986, s. 214).

Section 10 applies to the directors (but not shadow directors) of building societies; but it appears that this is so only in relation to wrongful, and not fraudulent trading: see ¶110 above.

On the application of s. 10 to the former members of insolvent partnerships, see ¶111 above.

No minimum period of disqualification is laid down; the normal maximum of 15 years applies (s. 10(2)).

Other points are noted in Chapters 5 and 6 below.

# 5 Directors' Personal Liability: Fraudulent Trading

## ¶501 Fraudulent trading

For many years the Companies Acts have made 'fraudulent trading' both a criminal offence (carrying up to seven years' imprisonment: see CA 1985, s. 458) and a ground for imposing personal liability upon those concerned (CA 1985, s. 630). Following the consolidation of the insolvency law in 1986, s. 458 remains in force, but s. 630 has been re-enacted (with amendments, see ¶505) as s. 213 of the Insolvency Act 1986. The civil provision, unlike the criminal offence, applies only in a winding-up. Section 213 has effect when 'in the course of the winding up of a company it appears that any business of the company has been carried on with intent to defraud creditors of the company or creditors of any other person, or for any fraudulent purpose'. Where this is found to be the case, the court may declare that those who were knowingly parties to the carrying on of the business in the manner described are to be liable to make such contributions to the company's assets as the court thinks proper, and it may also make a disqualification order against them (see ¶420 above).

## ¶502 Recommendations of the Cork Committee

The Cork Committee (*Report*, Chapter 44) considered that the law in this area was inadequate as it stood to deal with irresponsible trading, mainly because the courts insisted on the very strict standards of pleading and proof which are invariably applied in criminal proceedings and cases of fraud. It has never been enough to show that the company continued to run up debts when the directors knew that it was insolvent; there has to be 'actual dishonesty, involving real moral blame' (*Re Patrick & Lyon Ltd* [1933] Ch. 786). The Committee recommended that while this should continue to be the approach in *criminal* proceedings for fraudulent trading, *civil* liability to pay compensation could arise where loss was suffered as a result of 'unreasonable' conduct, which they proposed should be termed 'wrongful trading', and that for this purpose the more relaxed standard of proof appropriate to civil proceedings should apply.

## ¶503 Wrongful trading: the new law

The Insolvency Act 1985 introduced a regime making directors personally accountable for 'wrongful trading' which was broadly on the lines of the Cork proposals, with the following differences:

- it *supplemented* the 'fraudulent trading' provisions (s. 630 of the Companies Act 1985 (now IA 1986, s. 213)) instead of subsuming both concepts into one comprehensive new section;
- the Act contained no explicit definition of wrongful trading, as Cork had recommended;
- it was confined in its scope to directors (including 'shadow directors') and was not extended so as to include others who were party to the wrongful trading.

These reforms have been consolidated as ss. 214 and 215 of the Insolvency Act 1986.

## ¶504 Law on fraudulent trading to continue

The old law on fraudulent trading thus remains in force. However, there will now be little reason for liquidators to have recourse to it, since the new concept of wrongful trading, with its less onerous standard of proof, is wide enough to include all cases of fraudulent trading, and for all practical purposes the civil law consequences will be the same.

## ¶505 Remedies and procedure

The Insolvency Act 1985, by Sch. 6, para. 6(1), made three minor changes to the existing law on fraudulent trading, so as to bring it into line with the provisions of the new law on wrongful trading. These changes have been consolidated in ss. 213 and 215 of the Insolvency Act 1986.

First, the order which the court may now make declares the wrongdoers 'liable to make such contributions (if any) to the company's assets as the court thinks proper' (IA 1986, s. 213(2)). This makes it clear that any sums ordered to be paid must go into the general funds in the hands of the liquidator and be held for the benefit of the whole body of creditors. Under the previous wording of s. 630 of the Companies Act 1985, the court had power to order that a defendant should personally reimburse a particular creditor (*Re Cyona Distributors Ltd* [1967] Ch. 889). The reformers thought that this was undesirable, because it might encourage an individual creditor to put improper pressure upon directors to settle his claim personally.

The same reasoning lies behind the second amendment. Previously, an application could be made by any creditor, but it is now obligatory to channel all claims through the liquidator.

Thirdly, the court is given power to direct that, if a defendant in fraudulent trading proceedings is himself a creditor of the company, his own debt (with any interest due) shall be postponed in priority so that it ranks *after* all other debts owed by the company (IA 1986, s. 215).

## ¶506 Disqualification for participation in fraudulent trading

Where the court has made a contribution order under s. 213, it may also make a disqualification order against the person concerned (CDDA 1986, s. 10: see ¶420 above). Alternatively, a disqualification order may be made (whether or not a compensation order is also sought) under the Company Directors Disqualification Act 1986, s. 2 or s. 4: see ¶402 and ¶404.

## ¶507 Application to insolvent partnerships

The law on fraudulent trading extends to the members of insolvent partnerships, but not to the directors of building societies (see ¶110–¶111 above).

# 6 Directors' Personal Liability: 'Wrongful Trading'

## ¶601 The concept of wrongful trading

The concept of wrongful trading was introduced to supplement the law of fraudulent trading (see Chapter 5 above). However, because of the less demanding standard of proof, it is bound in practice inevitably to supersede it. The drafting of the new provision (IA 1986, s. 214) is, however, far from clear, and it is difficult to determine its precise scope. We know from all sorts of external sources – the Cork Report, *Hansard*, even the marginal note to the section – that it is intended to make directors personally liable for 'wrongful trading', but the words 'wrongful trading' do not appear in the substantive text of the section at all – nor even the word 'trading'. At this stage one can only guess at the interpretation which will ultimately be developed by case law.

The Cork Committee did put forward its own draft definition of 'wrongful trading' (*Report*, para. 1806), the essential part of which read:

> '. . . at any time when the company is insolvent or unable to pay its debts as they fall due it incurs further debts or other liabilities to other persons without a reasonable prospect of meeting them in full.'

However, this definition was explicitly rejected by Parliament when an attempt was made to introduce it as an amendment to the Bill in 1985, and so it would be quite wrong to refer to it for guidance on the meaning of s. 214. In particular, there may be wrongful trading under the section even though the company does not incur further debts: one example mentioned during the Parliamentary debate was the case where a company allows its assets to become depleted, e.g. by the payment of excessive directors' fees. It was, presumably, a concern to ensure that conduct of this sort was caught, quite as much as irresponsibility in running up further credit, that led the draftsman to omit even the word 'trading' from his formulation.

## ¶602 Marginal note irrelevant

In passing, it is perhaps worth noting that the rules of statutory interpretation state that a marginal note may not be used as an aid for the construction of legislation (*Chandler & Ors* v *Director of Public Prosecutions* [1964] AC 763); and so it is not legitimate to draw any inference from the words 'company's wrongful trading' in the side-note to s. 214.

## ¶603 The statutory definition

It appears that liability for 'wrongful trading' will arise when the following points are satisfied:

- the company has 'gone into insolvent liquidation';
- the person concerned is, or was at the relevant time, a director or shadow director;
- the person must at that time have known, or failed to realise when he ought to have done, that there was 'no reasonable prospect that the company would avoid going into insolvent liquidation'; and
- he thereafter failed to take 'every step with a view to minimising the potential loss to the company's creditors' as ought to have been taken.

This wide language, coupled with the more relaxed standard of pleading and proof which is now appropriate, clearly makes it very much easier for liquidators and the courts to deal with cases of blatantly reckless trading by irresponsible directors. In this task they are helped by the provisions of s. 214(4) and (5), which direct that the conduct of a director is to be judged by partly objective standards, thus making it possible to penalise incompetence, ignorance and indifference quite as much as conscious wrong-doing. However, the vagueness of the statutory text also creates the risk that conscientious and well-intentioned directors will, perhaps unwittingly, be caught by its terms.

It is surely a fair criticism to say that in its zeal to ensure that true delinquents do not escape their deserts, Parliament has failed to give any affirmative guidance as to what *is* to be regarded as acceptable conduct on the part of those directors (undoubtedly the great majority) whose only concern is to do their best for their company when it is in difficulties. It is not a complete answer to say that of course the courts will use their discretion, and decline to make a contribution order in a proper case, for a director threatened with personal liability under s. 214 (and a possible disqualification order in consequence) may well be under considerable pressure to make an out-of-court settlement. Further, many people may be discouraged from offering their services to the boards of companies which are in difficulties because it is unclear what risks they may be exposing themselves to under the section. For these reasons, it is to be hoped that the courts will take the earliest opportunity, in an appropriate test case, to give directors the positive guidance that Parliament has not provided. Despite these uncertainties, we must now attempt to examine the requirements of s. 214 in more detail.

## ¶604 The meaning of 'gone into insolvent liquidation'

This phrase, which is to be contrasted with the expression 'has become insolvent' used in s. 6 of the Company Directors Disqualification Act 1986 (see ¶407 above), applies only in a liquidation; it is immaterial whether this is a compulsory or voluntary liquidation. By s. 214(7), a company 'goes into insolvent liquidation' if it goes into liquidation at a time when its assets are insufficient for the payment of its debts and other liabilities and the expenses of the winding-up. The test of insolvency to be applied is thus on a 'balance sheet' rather than a 'liquidity' basis (the Cork recommendation (para. 1806) was that *either* should be sufficient). However, the Act gives no indication whether the company's assets are to be valued for this purpose on a 'going concern' rather than a 'break-up' basis, or whether contingent future liabilities are to be brought into the reckoning. It is submitted that it would be wrong to judge these matters with the wisdom of hindsight, if for instance it does happen that the assets have had to be sold up piecemeal in the winding-up which has resulted. The reference to 'going into insolvent liquidation' in relation to the making of business judgments in s. 214(2)(*b*) supports this contention, for the question of solvency would in that context surely have to be assessed on the basis of going-concern assumptions.

## ¶605 'A person who is or has been a director'

'Director' includes 'shadow director' (s. 214(7): for the meaning of this term, see ¶109). Thus a person who is not a director, but controls the acts of others who are, is within the section. This could include a parent company.

In *Re a Company No. 005009 of 1987* (1988) 4 BCC 424 the court ruled that a company's bank was capable of being included within the concept of a shadow director for the purposes of s. 214. It had commissioned a report from its own financial services section which had shown that the company was 'in low financial water'; and had then allegedly taken steps to secure the implementation by the company of various recommendations that the report had made. The court declined on these facts to hold that an allegation that the bank was a shadow director was 'obviously unsustainable'.

The person must have been a director at the time that the prospect of insolvent liquidation was known, or ought to have become apparent. This latter phrase suggests that a director who decides to resign office rather than wait for the worst to be revealed will not necessarily escape liability.

On the application of s. 214 to the directors of building societies and the former members of insolvent partnerships, see ¶110 and ¶111 above.

## ¶606 'At some time before the commencement of the winding-up'

This is the only reference to time in the section. There is no anterior time-limit, a cut-off date before which the conduct of a director will not be scrutinised. So the section may be applied where the liquidation does not occur until several years after the wrongful trading and (in theory, at least) even where it is not shown to have been causally linked with it.

The section does, on the other hand, define the *latest* date by which a person must have known (or ought to have concluded) that an insolvent liquidation was virtually inescapable: the 'commencement' of the winding-up. Nothing will turn on this when the liquidation is voluntary, since such a winding-up is deemed to commence at the time of the passing of the resolution for winding-up (IA 1986, s. 86), and this will also be the date when the company 'goes into liquidation' (see IA 1986, s. 247); but where the winding-up is by court order, the winding-up is deemed to have commenced at an earlier date – either at the time of the presentation of the petition or, if there has already been a resolution for voluntary winding-up before the petition is presented, at the time when the resolution for voluntary winding-up was passed (IA 1986, s. 129). It is thus conceivable that there will be rare cases in which a director escapes liability under the section because he (reasonably) remained unaware that insolvency was just around the corner until a winding-up petition was actually presented.

## ¶607 'Knew or ought to have concluded'

These words, from s. 214(2)(*b*), have to be read in conjunction with s. 214(4). This states that the facts which a director ought to know or ascertain and the conclusions which he ought to reach are those that would have come to the mind of a reasonably diligent person in his place; and for this purpose both an objective and a subjective test will apply: first, he must be assumed to have the general knowledge, skill and experience reasonably to be expected of any person carrying out the same functions; and, secondly, the court must take into account the general knowledge, skill and experience that he actually has. In other words, he is to be judged by the standards of the 'reasonable' director even though he himself is lacking or below-average in knowledge, skill or experience, but by his own higher standards if these are above average. There will, however, be scope for the courts to make some allowances in the case of, e.g., non-executive or part-time directors, since s. 214(4)(*a*) makes express reference to the particular functions that the particular director carries out.

In applying objective standards to the conduct of company directors in this way, the Insolvency Acts break new ground: the emphasis in the case law for over a century has always been on the need for honesty and conscientiousness rather than any degree of competence or diligence or skill (see, e.g. *Re City Equitable Fire Insurance Co. Ltd* [1925] Ch. 407). This change is underlined by s. 214(5), which puts sins of omission into the same category as sins of commission: if the director 'does not carry out' any functions which 'have been entrusted to him', he is to be judged by the same criteria as if he had. Again, this is a departure from the common law, which has never had effective sanctions to penalise passive defaults such as non-attendance at board meetings.

## ¶608 Director exonerated if he 'took every step with a view to minimising potential loss'

Section 214(3) is likely to prove a troublesome provision to apply in practice. The court is directed not to make a declaration of personal liability against a person if it is satisfied that, after the time when he first knew or ought to have known that there was no reasonable prospect of avoiding insolvent liquidation, he 'took every step with a view to minimising the potential loss to the company's creditors as he ought to have taken'; and for the purpose of determining what he 'ought' to have done, he is to be credited with an awareness of the company's financial position, and also with a degree of general knowledge, skill and experience which in reality he may not have had. This fictitious assumption as to the director's state of mind could well lead to many difficulties for the courts.

Next, there may be a problem concerning the onus of proof. It would be easy to assume that the Act requires the individual director to prove that he did all he could; but both on principle and on the language of the section it is submitted that it is for the liquidator to demonstrate to the court the steps that the director 'ought to have taken'.

The phrases 'took *every* step' and '*minimising* the potential loss to creditors' seem, at first sight, to overstate the obligation of the director, leaving him no margin for anything falling short of total compliance. However, there is no doubt that the use of 'every step' was deliberate: an amendment to 'every reasonable step' was expressly rejected in Parliament (although Lord Denning, in the debate, expressed the opinion that judges might in any case give the phrase this meaning). On similar reasoning, if the draftsman had intended to say 'reduce' or 'avert', rather than 'minimise', he could well have done so. Again, we must wait for judicial interpretation of the section.

## ¶609 Implications of the new law

There is a degree of novelty in the assumption which underlies this Part of the Act: that the primary duty of directors when their company appears to be in difficulties is to cut the potential loss to the company's *creditors*. The duty of directors under traditional company law is owed to the company, and the company alone (more precisely identified as the interests of its members and employees: see CA 1985, s. 309); and as recently as 1983 the courts in this country have denied the possibility that directors owe duties of any kind to creditors (*Multinational Gas and Petrochemical Co.* v *Multinational Gas and Petrochemical Services Ltd & Ors* [1983] Ch. 258). However, in the last year or two various judges appear to have endorsed the view that a different rule should apply in a situation of actual or threatening insolvency (see, e.g. *Winkworth* v *Edward Baron Development Co. Ltd & Ors* [1987] 1 All ER 114, at p. 118; (1987) 3 BCC 4, at p. 8, *Liquidator of West Mercia Safetywear Ltd* v *Dodd & Anor* (1988) 4 BCC 30, at p. 33). These statements, in recognising that the duties of directors when insolvency is imminent do include an obligation to have regard to the interests of their company's creditors, bring the case law and the legislation more or less into line.

This approach of the legislators is based on a rather more questionable assumption – that when insolvency is threatening the best deal for the company's creditors is most likely to be achieved by putting the company into voluntary liquidation or receivership, or seeking an administration order, as soon as possible (see the White Paper, Cmnd 9175, para. 12). All these proceedings are costly, and creditors may well fare worse in a forced sale of assets. It is surely a reasonable view that a conscientious board of directors should be entitled to have regard to these considerations, as well as to the implications of premature liquidation for the company's employees, trading partners, customers and perhaps even wider interests, and to strive to keep an ailing company afloat – even if it may mean chancing the claims of existing creditors and very possibly incurring further indebtedness. This may be the very moment when extra nerve is called for, and a willingness to take the ultimate in risks; but it is all too easy for others later to brand such conduct as over-optimistic and irresponsible if the worst does happen. Government spokesmen during the Parliamentary debate expressed their confidence that the judges would interpret the section in such a way as to let off directors who felt it was their duty to stay at the corporate helm rather than leave or scupper the sinking ship. It is to be hoped that the judges will find scope to do so, despite the fact that the section is expressed in such uncompromisingly objective and absolute terms. If they do not, then the fears which have been widely expressed – that the Act may deter company 'doctors' and discourage rescue attempts when companies are in difficulties – will prove to be well founded.

## ¶610 Practical consequences for directors

It will be essential for directors to ensure that they are at all times familiar with the financial affairs of their company, and especially for non-executive directors to monitor its position regularly. Steps should be taken to tighten up accounting procedures, and to see that the filing requirements of the Companies Acts are regularly complied with. The law has always tolerated a good deal of informality in the running of small companies, but it will be wise in future, at least in the case of companies which are not in abundant financial health, to make sure that regular and formal board meetings are held and that decisions are fully documented. Outside advice may have to be sought if the company's viability is in doubt, since an inexperienced director is unlikely to be regarded as having 'taken every step' if he simply remains inactive or trusts to the judgement of his colleagues. It will certainly be risky for a board unaided by experts to decide to continue trading on the basis of hunch or hope, for with hindsight such optimism may well not be given the benefit of the doubt.

If directors do discover that their company is insolvent, the Act gives them little affirmative guidance as to what they should do. Indeed, it is open to the serious criticism that, for want of such guidance, directors may panic and put their companies into premature receivership or liquidation rather than attempt to nurse them back to health. In order to avoid charges of 'wrongful trading', directors who do decide to soldier on should ensure that their decisions are fully reasoned and documented, based on sound evidence and, at least where the board itself is lacking in expertise, made with the benefit of good professional advice. Since the law extends to former directors as well as those in office at the commencement of the liquidation, it is plain that a director cannot escape liability by simply resigning as difficulties loom. However, for a minority director who has failed to persuade his colleagues to take what he believes are prudent or proper steps, there may be no course open other than to have his dissent recorded and step down. He has, after all, no standing on his own to apply for a winding-up or administration order or to initiate a voluntary arrangement.

There is the additional danger that those who are closely associated with an ailing company may be drawn into a situation of personal liability as 'shadow directors': for instance, a banker or a parent company (see ¶108). It will be important for anyone so placed to ensure that the company does not take any step on his instruction or direction that may increase the potential loss to its creditors.

## ¶611 Procedure

As has already been noted (see ¶505 above), only the liquidator has standing to make an application under s. 214.

Section 215 incorporates the various procedural innovations which now also apply in the case of fraudulent trading (see ¶505 above).

## ¶612 Application of payments

All sums ordered to be paid under this section go into the general funds in the hands of the liquidator; it is not open to the court to direct the wrongdoer to pay the amount of a particular debt to an individual creditor.

There is nothing in s. 214 which restricts the discretion of the court in fixing the amount of contribution that a director shall make. In particular, since liability is not made to depend upon the fact that a person was a party, or privy, to wrongful trading, the contribution is not limited to the amount of debts that were incurred during the period of wrongful trading: it may be more or less.

## ¶613 Disqualification on grounds of wrongful trading

A person who has been declared liable to make a contribution for wrongful trading under s. 214 may also, if the court thinks fit, have a disqualification order made against him (CDDA 1986, s. 10; see ¶420 above).

## ¶614 No anticipatory declarations

The proposal of the Cork Committee (*Report*, paras. 1798–1804) that it should be possible to make an application to the court while a company was a going concern for an anticipatory declaration that certain proposed trading would not be 'wrongful' was not taken up by the legislature.

## ¶615 The first judicial ruling on wrongful trading

Since this book went to press, judgment has been given in the first case decided under s. 214, *Re Produce Marketing Consortium Ltd* (Knox J, 22 March 1989, to be reported in (1989) 5 BCC 569). In this seminal ruling, two directors were held liable to contribute a total sum of £75,000 to their company's assets in its liquidation when, without dishonesty, they had allowed their company to continue trading for a further year after they ought to have realised that there was no reasonable prospect that it could avoid going into insolvent liquidation. For this purpose, they were deemed to have the knowledge of the financial position which would have been revealed if its results for the year had been produced at the end of the trading year as required by the Companies Act.

A more detailed summary of the judgment appears in Appendix 3 (see p. 88).

# 7 Directors' Personal Liability: Acting While Disqualified: Use of Prohibited Company Name

## ¶701 Personal liability for breach of disqualification order

Section 15 of the Company Directors Disqualification Act 1986 is designed to prevent a person against whom a disqualification order has been made from trading with the benefits of limited liability, directly or indirectly, while the disqualification order is in force. It applies also in relation to an undischarged bankrupt, who is prohibited by s. 11 from being involved in the management of a company. In addition, s. 15 seeks to discourage a disqualified person or undischarged bankrupt from using a 'front man' to run a company on his behalf, by making the 'front man' himself also personally liable for the debts incurred. There can be little doubt that this provision, in combination with the disqualification order and wrongful trading provisions discussed above, will be a powerful weapon to prevent the abuse of limited liability described as the 'phoenix syndrome' which was all too common prior to the insolvency reforms of 1985. Under this practice, a new company was incorporated by the former controllers of a defunct company to buy up the assets of the latter in its insolvent liquidation, usually at a knock-down price, so that what was essentially the same business could be carried on by the same people in disregard of the claims of the unpaid creditors of the first company. In some notorious instances, this procedure was repeated several times.

## ¶702 Who is liable?

Section 15(1)(*a*) makes anyone who is involved in the management of a company in contravention of a disqualification order (or of s. 11) personally responsible for all the debts of the company that are incurred during the relevant time. Liability is imposed automatically by the law, without the need for any court order. The phrase 'involved in the management of a company' is elaborated in s. 15(4) and (5); for this purpose cases such as *R* v *Austen* and *R* v *Campbell* (see ¶201 above) will be relevant. Section 15(1)(*b*) is aimed at the 'front man' described above, who will similarly incur personal liability if he acts or is 'willing to act' on the instructions of a banned person, unless the court grants him special dispensation. Liability will be incurred by a 'front man' from the time that he first knows that the other is a banned person; and once he is shown to have acted knowingly for a banned person in the management of a company on a particular occasion, he will become prima facie liable for all the company's obligations incurred at any time thereafter, for the Act sets up a (rebuttable) presumption that he has continued 'willing to act' on that person's instructions (s. 15(3), (5)).

It is immaterial for the purposes of s. 15 whether the involvement of a person in the management of a company is direct or indirect (s. 15(4)).

Liability will extend not only to debts in the narrow sense but also to all other obligations, such as claims for damages, and it applies to all obligations arising during the relevant time and not merely those incurred *by* the acts of the person in question.

Section 15(2) declares that where a person is personally responsible for the debts of a company under s. 15, he is jointly and severally liable in respect of those debts with the company and with any other person who may be liable for the same debts. This means that a creditor may sue the company and all or any such persons, or any combination of them, for the whole debt and, if he is successful, enter judgment against each of them for the entire amount. He may then enforce the judgment against any one or more of them until it is satisfied in full. Where one of several joint and several debtors has been obliged to pay a debt, he may seek contribution from any one or more of the others in proceedings brought under the Civil Liability (Contribution) Act 1978, and the court may in its discretion order a contribution to be made, or even award a complete indemnity. It is possible, therefore, that a director who is personally liable under the Company Directors Disqualification Act 1986, s. 15 may obtain reimbursement from his company, but this of course will be of no avail if the company is insolvent.

## ¶703 Re-use of prohibited company name

Section 216 of the Insolvency Act 1986 (formerly IA 1985, s. 17) places restrictions on the re-use (except with the leave of the court) of a 'prohibited' company name by its former directors for a period of five years after that company has gone into insolvent liquidation. In addition to the criminal sanctions prescribed by s. 216 itself, s. 217 imposes personal liability on the directors and other persons who are involved in the management of the successor business that uses the prohibited name. This is done in terms which are virtually identical with s. 15 of the Company Directors Disqualification

Act 1986 (see ¶701 above). In particular, the phrases 'go into insolvent liquidation', 'involved in the management of a company', 'relevant debts' and 'acts or is willing to act on instructions given' are defined in the same terms in the two sections, and the presumptions and other rules of liability as regards a 'front man' are an exact parallel.

A company name is a 'prohibited' name if it is a name by which the insolvent company had been known at any time within the 12 months before it went into liquidation, or is a name so similar as to suggest an association with that company. In addition to its registered name, a company may be 'known by' any name under which it carries on business – e.g. a trade name.

The court is empowered to grant dispensations from the prohibition imposed by s. 216, which it is likely to do when the insolvency is not linked with any blameworthy conduct on the part of the director concerned. Section 216(3) also allows exemptions from the ban on the re-use of names in certain circumstances to be prescribed by subordinate legislation. This has been done by the Insolvency Rules 1986, rr. 4.228–4.230. Three sets of circumstances have been specified. These are:

- where the whole, or substantially the whole, of the business of an insolvent company is acquired by a successor company and the liquidator (or other insolvency practitioner concerned) gives notice in prescribed form to its creditors (r. 4.228);
- for an interim period, where an application is made to the court within seven days of the liquidation and the court grants leave not later than six weeks from that date (r. 4.229);
- where the second company has been known by the name in question for at least 12 months prior to the liquidation and has not been a dormant company (r. 4.230).

## ¶704 Extension to directors of building societies

The prohibition on the re-use of prohibited names extends to the directors of building societies: see ¶110 above.

## ¶705 Applications for leave to use a prohibited name

Some applications for leave to use a prohibited name have been unofficially reported (see Graham Harp, *Insolvency Intelligence*, Vol. 1, at pp. 65ff).

In the case of *British Dental Floss* (13 June 1988), the court was satisfied that the failure of the previous company was due to misfortune rather than misconduct and granted leave without any conditions. The court expressed the view that the appropriate procedure was by *ex parte* application, but that notice should be given to the Secretary of State or official receiver so that he might, if he wished, exercise his right to appear; however, unless there was some relevant information about the failed company to be brought to the attention of the court, the Secretary of State or official receiver should not normally exercise that right but might instead simply write to the court stating that there was nothing to be drawn to the court's attention.

In *Oasis Marketing Ltd* (18 June 1988), the court said that the sections were clearly protective rather than penal and that the court therefore needed to look at the applicant's conduct in the failed company in much the same way as in a disqualification application. On the evidence, it was satisfied that the applicant's conduct did not give cause for concern and granted the application.

In *Pestroyed Preservations (Ewell) Ltd* (24 May 1988), the applicants sought and were granted limited leave to act for two months in order to dispose of companies with prohibited names. The court called for a report from the liquidator and he was granted his costs.

# 8 Directors' Personal Liability Under the Companies Act 1985

## ¶801 Introduction

In this chapter are examined certain provisions of the Companies Act 1985 under which a director may incur personal liability for his company's debts or other obligations, thus losing the protection of limited liability. Some of these provisions may apply to a wider category of persons and not simply to directors, but even so it is directors who are most likely to be caught by the section in question.

Of course, a director may incur personal liability to his company, its shareholders or outside parties in any number of ways. The present discussion, however, concentrates on the narrower range of statutorily imposed liabilities for obligations which are, at least prima facie, those of the company; and it is confined to civil liability.

## ¶802 Liability upon cheques, etc. on which company's name is wrongly stated

Section 349(4) of the Companies Act 1985 states that a director or other officer of a company is personally liable to the holder of a bill of exchange, promissory note, endorsement, cheque or order for money or goods (unless it is duly paid by the company) if:

- he has signed or authorised the signing of the document on behalf of the company; and
- the company's name is not mentioned on the document in legible characters.

In practice, a director will be likely to incur personal liability under this provision (usually on a cheque) because the company's name has not been stated *accurately*, and in many cases the inaccuracy will consist of the omission of the word 'Limited' (or the abbreviation 'Ltd' or, if appropriate, 'plc'). The company, of course, will normally also be liable on the document as a primary party, so that the director's obligation is of a secondary character.

Two recent cases illustrate the operation of this provision. In *Blum* v *O.C.P. Repartition S.A.* (1988) 4 BCC 771, a director had signed seven cheques bearing the personalised name of his company without the word 'Limited'; the company was put into liquidation and its bank refused to make payment. The director was held to be personally liable. A similar conclusion was reached in *Lindholst & Co. A/S* v *Fowler & Anor* (1988) 4 BCC 776, despite the fact that it was the other party to the contract who had put forward the bills of exchange in question and had itself wrongly written the company's name for acceptance. The court took the view that it was the duty of the director to see that the acceptance was in proper form before he signed it.

## ¶803 Liability where public company commences business prematurely

Section 117 of the Companies Act 1985 imposes conditions as to the minimum share capital of a public company, and forbids such a company to do business or exercise any borrowing powers unless the registrar is satisfied that the capital requirements have been met and has issued a certificate accordingly. If a company enters into a transaction in contravention of the section and fails to comply with its obligations in that connection within 21 days of being called upon to do so, the directors are jointly and severally liable to indemnify the other party to the transaction in respect of any loss or damage suffered by him.

## ¶804 Directors' personal liability where shares are purchased or redeemed out of capital

A private company may in certain circumstances redeem or repurchase its shares out of capital, following the procedure prescribed by the Companies Act 1985, ss. 173ff. For this purpose, the directors are required to make a statutory declaration that the company is, in their opinion, solvent and will remain so throughout the ensuing year. If the company is wound up insolvent within one year of the date of the redemption or repurchase, the former shareholder and the directors are liable to contribute to the deficiency in the company's assets to an amount up to the sum paid by the company for the redemption or repurchase of the shares (IA 1986, s. 76).

# 9 Applications for Leave to Act as a Director During a Disqualification Order

## ¶901 Statutory provisions

Section 1 of the Company Directors Disqualification Act 1986 defines a disqualification order as an order that the person concerned shall not, *without the leave of the court*, be a director, etc. of a company. In a similar way, s. 11 of the same Act makes it an offence for an undischarged bankrupt to act as a director, etc. of a company, *except with the leave of the court.*

There is little case law to throw light on the practice of the courts in granting leave under either of these sections or, indeed, to indicate whether the same criteria will be applied in the exercise of jurisdiction under the two provisions. However, in relation to an application for leave made by an undischarged bankrupt, Murray J (in *Re McQuillan* (1989) 5 BCC 137, a case decided in the Northern Ireland High Court) quoted with approval from the judgment of Street J in the Australian case of *Re Altim Pty. Ltd* [1968] 2 NSWR 762, at p. 764:

> 'The section under which this application is made proceeds upon the basis that a person who is an undischarged bankrupt is prima facie not to be permitted to act as a director or to take part in the management of a company. The court is given jurisdiction to grant leave for such activities to be carried on, but an applicant who comes to the court seeking leave must bear the onus of establishing that the general policy of the legislature laid down in this section ought to be made the subject of an exception in his case. It should be borne in mind that the section is not in any sense a punishment of the bankrupt. Nor should a refusal to grant leave under that section be regarded as punitive. The prohibition is entirely protective, and the power of the court to grant leave is to be exercised with this consideration in the forefront.'

## ¶902 Time and mode of application

An application may be made either during the currency of a disqualification order or, it would seem, at the time of the original hearing when the order is made. In the latter case, the disqualification order is in effect made subject to a proviso which allows the disqualified person to act in specified ways notwithstanding the order. In this latter case it is normal for the respondent, after he has been served with notice of the disqualification proceedings, to issue a notice of application asking for the leave in question, but it is understood that this pro forma request is sometimes dispensed with (e.g. in *Re Majestic Recording Studios Ltd & Ors* (1988) 4 BCC 519, an unreported part of the judgment).

## ¶903 Court to which application is made

It is not necessary that leave be granted by the same court as made the original order. Section 17 of the Company Directors Disqualification Act 1986 provides that where the application is for leave to promote or form a company, the appropriate court is 'any court with jurisdiction to wind up companies', while for an application for leave to be a liquidator, administrator or director of a company or a receiver, or to take part in its management, the appropriate court is 'any court having jurisdiction to wind up that company'.

## ¶904 Procedure

It is the duty of the Secretary of State, the official receiver or the liquidator on whose application the disqualification order was made to appear on the hearing of an application for leave and to call the attention of the court to any matters which seem to him to be relevant.

## ¶905 Conditions

The decided cases show that leave to act as a director, etc. may be given subject to conditions. In *Re Lo-Line Electric Motors Ltd & Ors* [1988] Ch. 477; (1988) 4 BCC 415, leave was granted to the respondent to be a director of two family companies so long as (i) a named relative, who was primarily responsible for the financial management of the businesses (and had, in the court's view, show himself to be capable and responsible), remained a director, and (ii) that relative and his family had voting control (in one case indirectly) of the two companies. In *Re Majestic Recording Studios Ltd & Ors* (1988) 4 BCC 519, leave was given to act as a director of one specified company if and for so long as the respondent had with him as co-director an independent chartered accountant approved by the court who was willing to act with him. It was also made a pre-condition of granting leave that audited accounts for the previous financial year be filed with the registrar.

In *Re D. J. Matthews (Joinery Design) Ltd & Anor* (1988) 4 BCC 513, it was hinted that the court might be more prepared to consider granting a disqualified person leave to act as a director of a company if it was an unlimited company and he was willing to assume unlimited personal liability; but this would only be taken into account, along with other matters of which evidence might be given, when the application was actually heard.

# 10 Insolvency Practitioners and Their Role

## ¶1001 Requirement that insolvency practitioners should be qualified

The insolvency legislation of 1985–86 introduced for the first time in this country a requirement that all insolvency practitioners should be licensed and bonded, and qualified to act in relation to the company in question. It is an offence for any person (other than the official receiver) to act as a liquidator, administrator or administrative receiver or as supervisor of a company voluntary arrangement without being so qualified.

## ¶1002 Duty of insolvency practitioner to report on conduct of directors of insolvent company

Section 7(3) of the Company Directors Disqualification Act 1986 requires the relevant office-holder to make a report to the Secretary of State on the conduct of any director or ex-director of an insolvent company, if it appears that that conduct makes him 'unfit' to be a director under the provisions of the Company Directors Disqualification Act 1986, s. 6(1). The office-holders specified in s. 7(3) are:

- in the case of a company which is being wound up by the court in England and Wales, the official receiver;
- in the case of a company which is being wound up otherwise, the liquidator;
- in the case of a company in relation to which an administration order is in force, the administrator;
- in the case of a company of which there is an administrative receiver, that receiver.

The section makes no mention of the supervisor of a voluntary arrangement.

Section 7(4) obliges the office-holder to furnish information and produce supporting documents, etc. to the Secretary of State on request.

Rules were made under the Insolvency Act 1985 to reinforce these requirements. These have now been re-issued as the Insolvent Companies

(Reports on Conduct of Directors) No. 2 Rules 1986 (SI 1986 No. 2134) and the Insolvent Companies (Reports on Conduct of Directors) (No. 2) (Scotland) Rules 1986 (SI 1986 No. 1916 (S. 140)). These rules impose an obligation on the insolvency practitioner concerned to complete and return prescribed forms in a number of stipulated cases. In England and Wales, the rules apply to:

(1) a creditors' voluntary winding-up;

(2) a voluntary winding-up which began as a members' voluntary winding-up but has proved to be insolvent; and

(3) an administrative receivership.

In Scotland, the rules apply in every winding-up and administrative receivership. Interim returns are also prescribed, to be made when the liquidation or receivership runs for more than six months. Fines may be imposed on a liquidator or administrative receiver who fails to comply, but – quite as importantly – an office-holder who is in breach of these reporting requirements may find that his authorisation to act as an insolvency practitioner is in jeopardy.

Some sample forms prescribed for the purposes of these rules are included in Appendix IV.

The original sets of rules became operative on 28 April 1986 and the reissued rules on 29 December 1986.

# 11 Transitional Provisions

## ¶1101 The new legislation: commencement dates

The director disqualification and wrongful trading provisions of the Insolvency Act 1985 (ss. 12–16, 18 and Sch. 2) came into force on 28 April 1986. In the consolidating legislation of 1986, these provisions have been re-enacted as ss. 6–10 and Sch. 1 of the Company Directors Disqualification Act 1986 and s. 214 of the Insolvency Act 1986.

The other sections of the new insolvency legislation of 1985 and 1986 which are discussed in this book became operative on 29 December 1986.

Certain provisions of the Company Directors Disqualification Act 1986 and the Insolvency Act 1986 were extended to the directors of building societies by the Building Societies Act 1986 (see ¶110 above). This amendment took effect from 1 January 1987.

## ¶1102 Transitional provisions: events before 28 April 1986

The provisions of the Insolvency Act 1985 which were brought into force on 28 April 1986 (see ¶1101 above) did not operate retrospectively so as to apply to events before that date (IA 1985, Sch. 9). This situation is continued by the consolidating legislation. In particular, the following points may be noted:

(1) *Disqualification of unfit directors of insolvent companies* (CDDA 1986, s. 6). If a company went into liquidation before 28 April 1986, the court is not to make a disqualification order against any of its directors or former directors unless it could have done so under the repealed s. 300 of the Companies Act 1985 (CDDA 1986, Sch. 2, para. 7).

(2) *Disqualification after investigation of company* (CDDA 1986, s. 8). A disqualification order may not be made on the basis of a report made by inspectors to the Secretary of State for Trade and Industry, or of information or documents obtained by him, before 28 April 1986 (CDDA 1986, Sch. 2, para. 8).

(3) *Liability for wrongful trading*. The wrongful trading provisions of s. 214 of the Insolvency Act 1986 (formerly IA 1985, s. 15) do not apply where the company in question went into insolvent liquidation before 28 April 1986 (IA 1986, s. 214(2), IA 1985, Sch. 9, para. 4).

## ¶1103 Transitional provisions: director disqualification

Certain of the director disqualification provisions now found in ss. 2–5 of the Company Directors Disqualification Act 1986 were first introduced, or were substantially modified, by the Companies Act 1981 with effect from 15 June 1982. For example, the maximum disqualification period following conviction for an indictable offence (now CDDA 1986, s. 2) was increased from five to fifteen years. These changes did not operate retrospectively. Schedule 2 of the Company Directors Disqualification Act 1986, paras. 1–4 and 6 preserves all these features of the former law. For details, reference should be made to this Schedule.

## ¶1104 Transitional provisions: offences and default orders before 1 June 1977

For the purposes of ss. 3(1) and 5 of the Company Directors Disqualification Act 1986, no account is to be taken of any offence which was committed, or any default order which was made, before 1 June 1977 (CDDA 1986, Sch. 2, para. 5).

## ¶1105 Other transitional provisions

All the sections of the Companies Act 1985 which have been consolidated, and those sections of the Insolvency Act 1985 which were already in force on 29 December 1986 (when they were superseded by IA 1986 and CDDA 1986), are in substance continued under the corresponding provisions of the new legislation (IA 1986, Sch. 11, paras. 23–5; CDDA 1986, Sch. 3, paras. 2–4). No detailed transitional arrangements were required to deal with any matters falling under these provisions, except that some of the subordinate legislation relating to the former law has been re-enacted so as to bring the relevant statutory references up to date (e.g. the regulations obliging office-holders to report on the conduct of directors: see Chapter 10).

The other provisions of the 1986 Acts do not apply retrospectively.

# Appendix I: Text of Relevant Statutory Provisions

Sections 213–217 of the Insolvency Act 1986, and all the provisions of the Company Directors Disqualification Act 1986 are reproduced below. The notes in square brackets have been added by CCH Editions Limited.

## INSOLVENCY ACT 1986

### Section 213 Fraudulent trading

**213(1) [Application]** If in the course of the winding up of a company it appears that any business of the company has been carried on with intent to defraud creditors of the company or creditors of any other person, or for any fraudulent purpose, the following has effect.

**213(2) [Court may hold persons liable]** The court, on the application of the liquidator may declare that any persons who were knowingly parties to the carrying on of the business in the manner above-mentioned are to be liable to make such contributions (if any) to the company's assets as the court thinks proper.

### Section 214 Wrongful trading

**214(1) [Declaration by court, on application]** Subject to subsection (3) below, if in the course of the winding up of a company it appears that subsection (2) of this section applies in relation to a person who is or has been a director of the company, the court, on the application of the liquidator, may declare that that person is to be liable to make such contribution (if any) to the company's assets as the court thinks proper.

**214(2) [Application]** This subsection applies in relation to a person if—

(a) the company has gone into insolvent liquidation,

(b) at some time before the commencement of the winding up of the company, that person knew or ought to have concluded that there was no reasonable prospect that the company would avoid going into insolvent liquidation, and

(c) that person was a director of the company at that time;

but the court shall not make a declaration under this section in any case where the time mentioned in paragraph (b) above was before 28th April 1986.

**214(3) [Limit on declaration]** The court shall not make a declaration under this section with respect to any person if it is satisfied that after the condition specified in subsection (2)(b) was first satisfied in relation to him that person took every step with a view to minimising the potential loss to the company's creditors as (assuming him to have known that there was no reasonable prospect that the company would avoid going into insolvent liquidation) he ought to have taken.

**214(4) [Interpretation of s. 214(2), (3)]** For the purposes of subsections (2) and (3), the facts which a director of a company ought to know or ascertain, the conclusions which he ought to reach and the steps which he ought to take are those which would be known or ascertained, or reached or taken, by a reasonably diligent person having both—

(a) the general knowledge, skill and experience that may reasonably be expected of a person carrying out the same functions as are carried out by that director in relation to the company, and

(b) the general knowledge, skill and experience that that director has.

**214(5) [Interpretation of s. 214(4)]** The reference in subsection (4) to the functions carried out in relation to a company by a director of the company includes any functions which he does not carry out but which have been entrusted to him.

**214(6) [Interpretation re insolvent liquidation]** For the purposes of this section a company goes into insolvent liquidation if it goes into liquidation at a time when its assets are insufficient for the payment of its debts and other liabilities and the expenses of the winding up.

**214(7) [''Director'']** In this section **''director''** includes a shadow director.

**214(8) [S. 213]** This section is without prejudice to section 213.

## Section 215 Proceedings under ss. 213, 214

**215(1) [Evidence by liquidator]** On the hearing of an application under section 213 or 214, the liquidator may himself give evidence or call witnesses.

**215(2) [Further court directions]** Where under either section the court makes a declaration, it may give such further directions as it thinks proper for giving effect to the declaration; and in particular, the court may—

(a) provide for the liability of any person under the declaration to be a charge on any debt or obligation due from the company to him, or on any mortgage or charge or any interest in a mortgage or charge on assets of the company held by or vested in him, or any person on his behalf, or any person claiming as assignee from or through the person liable or any person acting on his behalf, and

(b) from time to time make such further order as may be necessary for enforcing any charge imposed under this subsection.

**215(3) [''Assignee']** For the purposes of subsection (2), **''assignee''**—

(a) includes a person to whom or in whose favour, by the directions of the person made liable, the debt, obligation, mortgage or charge was created, issued or transferred or the interest created, but

(b) does not include an assignee for valuable consideration (not including consideration by way of marriage) given in good faith and without notice of any of the matters on the ground of which the declaration is made.

**215(4) [Directions re priority of debts]** Where the court makes a declaration under either section in relation to a person who is a creditor of the company, it may direct that the whole or any part of any debt owed by the company to that person and any interest thereon shall rank in priority after all other debts owed by the company and after any interest on those debts.

**215(5) [Ss. 213, 214]** Sections 213 and 214 have effect notwithstanding that the person concerned may be criminally liable in respect of matters on the ground of which the declaration under the section is to be made.

## Section 216 Restriction on re-use of company names

**216(1) [Application]** This section applies to a person where a company (**"the liquidating company"**) has gone into insolvent liquidation on or after the appointed day and he was a director or shadow director of the company at any time in the period of 12 months ending with the day before it went into liquidation.

**216(2) [Prohibited name]** For the purposes of this section, a name is a prohibited name in relation to such a person if—

(a) it is a name by which the liquidating company was known at any time in that period of 12 months, or

(b) it is a name which is so similar to a name falling within paragraph (a) as to suggest an association with that company.

**216(3) [Restriction]** Except with leave of the court or in such circumstances as may be prescribed, a person to whom this section applies shall not at any time in the period of 5 years beginning with the day on which the liquidating company went into liquidation—

(a) be a director of any other company that is known by a prohibited name, or

(b) in any way, whether directly or indirectly, be concerned or take part in the promotion, formation or management of any such company, or

(c) in any way, whether directly or indirectly, be concerned or take part in the carrying on of a business carried on (otherwise than by a company) under a prohibited name.

**216(4) [Penalty]** If a person acts in contravention of this section, he is liable to imprisonment or a fine, or both.

**216(5) ["The court"]** In subsection (3) **"the court"** means any court having jurisdiction to wind up companies; and on an application for leave under that subsection, the Secretary of State or the official receiver may appear and call the attention of the court to any matters which seem to him to be relevant.

**216(6) [Interpretation re name]** References in this section, in relation to any time, to a name by which a company is known are to the name of the company at that time or to any name under which the company carries on business at that time.

**216(7) [Interpretation re insolvent liquidation]** For the purposes of this section a company goes into insolvent liquidation if it goes into liquidation at a time when its assets are insufficient for the payment of its debts and other liabilities and the expenses of the winding up.

**216(8) ["Company"]** In this section "**company**" includes a company which may be wound up under Part V of this Act.

## Section 217 Personal liability for debts, following contravention of s. 216

**217(1) [Personal liability]** A person is personally responsible for all the relevant debts of a company if at any time—

(a) in contravention of section 216, he is involved in the management of the company, or

(b) as a person who is involved in the management of the company, he acts or is willing to act on instructions given (without the leave of the court) by a person whom he knows at that time to be in contravention in relation to the company of section 216.

**217(2) [Joint and several liability]** Where a person is personally responsible under this section for the relevant debts of a company, he is jointly and severally liable in respect of those debts with the company and any other person who, whether under this section or otherwise, is so liable.

**217(3) [Relevant debts of company]** For the purposes of this section the relevant debts of a company are—

(a) in relation to a person who is personally responsible under paragraph (a) of subsection (1), such debts and other liabilities of the company as are incurred at a time when that person was involved in the management of the company, and

(b) in relation to a person who is personally responsible under paragraph (b) of that subsection, such debts and other liabilities of the company as are incurred at a time when that person was acting or was willing to act on instructions given as mentioned in that paragraph.

**217(4) [Person involved in management]** For the purposes of this section, a person is involved in the management of a company if he is a director of the company or if he is concerned, whether directly or indirectly, or takes part, in the management of the company.

**217(5) [Interpretation]** For the purposes of this section a person who, as a person involved in the management of a company, has at any time acted on instructions given (without the leave of the court) by a person whom he knew at that time to be in contravention in relation to the company of section 216 is presumed, unless the contrary is shown, to have been willing at any time thereafter to act on any instructions given by that person.

**217(6) ["Company"]** In this section "**company**" includes a company which may be wound up under Part V.

# COMPANY DIRECTORS DISQUALIFICATION ACT 1986

PRELIMINARY

## Section 1 Disqualification orders: general

**1(1) [Disqualification order]** In the circumstances specified below in this Act a court may, and under section 6 shall, make against a person a disqualification order, that is to say an order that he shall not, without leave of the court—

(a) be a director of a company, or

(b) be a liquidator or administrator of a company, or

(c) be a receiver or manager of a company's property, or

(d) in any way, whether directly or indirectly, be concerned or take part in the promotion, formation or management of a company,

for a specified period beginning with the date of the order.

**1(2) [Maximum, minimum periods]** In each section of this Act which gives to a court power or, as the case may be, imposes on it the duty to make a disqualification order there is specified the maximum (and, in section 6, the minimum) period of disqualification which may or (as the case may be) must be imposed by means of the order.

**1(3) [Where two orders]** Where a disqualification order is made against a person who is already subject to such an order, the periods specified in those orders shall run concurrently.

**1(4) [Criminal grounds]** A disqualification order may be made on grounds which are or include matters other than criminal convictions, notwithstanding that the person in respect of whom it is to be made may be criminally liable in respect of those matters.

DISQUALIFICATION FOR GENERAL MISCONDUCT IN CONNECTION WITH COMPANIES

## Section 2 Disqualification on conviction of indictable offence

**2(1) [Court's power]** The court may make a disqualification order against a person where he is convicted of an indictable offence (whether on indictment or summarily) in connection with the promotion, formation, management or liquidation of a company, or with the receivership or management of a company's property.

**2(2) ["The court"]** **"The court"** for this purpose means—

(a) any court having jurisdiction to wind up the company in relation to which the offence was committed, or

(b) the court by or before which the person is convicted of the offence, or

(c) in the case of a summary conviction in England and Wales, any other magistrates' court acting for the same petty sessions area;

and for the purposes of this section the definition of **"indictable offence"** in Schedule 1 to the Interpretation Act 1978 applies for Scotland as it does for England and Wales.

**2(3) [Maximum period]** The maximum period of disqualification under this section is—

(a) where the disqualification order is made by a court of summary jurisdiction, 5 years, and

(b) in any other case, 15 years.

## Section 3 Disqualification for persistent breaches of companies legislation

**3(1) [Court's power]** The court may make a disqualification order against a person where it appears to it that he has been persistently in default in relation to provisions of the companies legislation requiring any return, account or other document to be filed with, delivered or sent, or notice of any matter to be given, to the registrar of companies.

**3(2) [Conclusive proof of default]** On an application to the court for an order to be made under this section, the fact that a person has been persistently in default in relation to such provisions as are mentioned above may (without prejudice to its proof in any other manner) be conclusively proved by showing that in the 5 years ending with the date of the application he has been adjudged guilty (whether or not on the same occasion) of three or more defaults in relation to those provisions.

**3(3) [Guilty of default under s. 3(2)]** A person is to be treated under subsection (2) as being adjudged guilty of a default in relation to any provision of that legislation if—

(a) he is convicted (whether on indictment or summarily) of an offence consisting in a contravention of or failure to comply with that provision (whether on his own part or on the part of any company), or

(b) a default order is made against him, that is to say an order under any of the following provisions—

(i) section 244 of the Companies Act (order requiring delivery of company accounts),

(ii) section 713 of that Act (enforcement of company's duty to make returns),

(iii) section 41 of the Insolvency Act (enforcement of receiver's or manager's duty to make returns), or

(iv) section 170 of that Act (corresponding provision for liquidator in winding up),

in respect of any such contravention of or failure to comply with that provision (whether on his own part or on the part of any company).

**3(4) [“The court”]** In this section **“the court”** means any court having jurisdiction to wind up any of the companies in relation to which the offence or other default has been or is alleged to have been committed.

**3(5) [Maximum period]** The maximum period of disqualification under this section is 5 years.

## Section 4 Disqualification for fraud, etc., in winding up

**4(1) [Court’s power]** The court may make a disqualification order against a person if, in the course of the winding up of a company, it appears that he—

(a) has been guilty of an offence for which he is liable (whether he has been convicted or not) under section 458 of the Companies Act (fraudulent trading), or

(b) has otherwise been guilty, while an officer or liquidator of the company or receiver or manager of its property, of any fraud in relation to the company or of any breach of his duty as such officer, liquidator, receiver or manager.

**4(2) [Definitions]** In this section **“the court”** means any court having jurisdiction to wind up any of the companies in relation to which the offence or other default has been or is alleged to have been committed; and **“officer”** includes a shadow director.

**4(3) [Maximum period]** The maximum period of disqualification under this section is 15 years.

## Section 5 Disqualification on summary conviction

**5(1) [Relevant offences]** An offence counting for the purposes of this section is one of which a person is convicted (either on indictment or summarily) in consequence of a contravention of, or failure to comply with, any provision of the companies legislation requiring a return, account or other document to be filed with, delivered or sent, or notice of any matter to be given, to the registrar of companies (whether the contravention or failure is on the person’s own part or on the part of any company).

**5(2) [Court’s power]** Where a person is convicted of a summary offence counting for those purposes, the court by which he is convicted (or, in England and Wales, any other magistrates’ court acting for the same petty sessions area) may make a disqualification order against him if the circumstances specified in the next subsection are present.

**5(3) [Circumstances in s. 5(2)]** Those circumstances are that, during the 5 years ending with the date of the conviction, the person has had made against him, or has been convicted of, in total not less than 3 default orders and offences counting for the purposes of this section; and those offences may include that of which he is convicted as mentioned in subsection (2) and any other offence of which he is convicted on the same occasion.

**5(4) [Definitions]** For the purposes of this section—

(a) the definition of "**summary offence**" in Schedule 1 to the Interpretation Act 1978 applies for Scotland as for England and Wales, and

(b) "**default order**" means the same as in section 3(3)(b).

**5(5) [Maximum period]** The maximum period of disqualification under this section is 5 years.

DISQUALIFICATION FOR UNFITNESS

## Section 6 Duty of court to disqualify unfit directors of insolvent companies

**6(1) [Court's duty]** The court shall make a disqualification order against a person in any case where, on an application under this section, it is satisfied—

(a) that he is or has been a director of a company which has at any time become insolvent (whether while he was a director or subsequently), and

(b) that his conduct as a director of that company (either taken alone or taken together with his conduct as a director of any other company or companies) makes him unfit to be concerned in the management of a company.

**6(2) [Interpretation]** For the purposes of this section and the next, a company becomes insolvent if—

(a) the company goes into liquidation at a time when its assets are insufficient for the payment of its debts and other liabilities and the expenses of the winding up,

(b) an administration order is made in relation to the company, or

(c) an administrative receiver of the company is appointed;

and references to a person's conduct as a director of any company or companies include, where that company or any of those companies has become insolvent, that person's conduct in relation to any matter connected with or arising out of the insolvency of that company.

**6(3) [Definitions]** In this section and the next "**the court**" means—

(a) in the case of a person who is or has been a director of a company which is being wound up by the court, the court by which the company is being wound up,

(b) in the case of a person who is or has been a director of a company which is being wound up voluntarily, any court having jurisdiction to wind up the company,

(c) in the case of a person who is or has been a director of a company in relation to which an administration order is in force, the court by which that order was made, and

(d) in any other case, the High Court or, in Scotland, the Court of Session;

and in both sections "**director**" includes a shadow director.

**6(4) [Minimum, maximum periods]** Under this section the minimum period of disqualification is 2 years, and the maximum period is 15 years.

**Note**
See important CCH Note after s. 7.

## Section 7 Applications to court under s. 6; reporting provisions

**7(1) [Application by Secretary of State, official receiver]** If it appears to the Secretary of State that it is expedient in the public interest that a disqualification order under section 6 should be made against any person, an application for the making of such an order against that person may be made—

(a) by the Secretary of State, or

(b) if the Secretary of State so directs in the case of a person who is or has been a director of a company which is being wound up by the court in England and Wales, by the official receiver.

**Note**
For details, see the Insolvent Companies (Disqualification of Unfit Directors) Proceedings Rules 1986 (SI 1986 No. 612).

**7(2) [Time for application]** Except with the leave of the court, an application for the making under that section of a disqualification order against any person shall not be made after the end of the period of 2 years beginning with the day on which the company of which that person is or has been a director became insolvent.

**7(3) [Report to Secretary of State]** If it appears to the office-holder responsible under this section, that is to say—

(a) in the case of a company which is being wound up by the court in England and Wales, the official receiver,

(b) in the case of a company which is being wound up otherwise, the liquidator,

(c) in the case of a company in relation to which an administration order is in force, the administrator, or

(d) in the case of a company of which there is an administrative receiver, that receiver,

that the conditions mentioned in section 6(1) are satisfied as respects a person who is or has been a director of that company, the office-holder shall forthwith report the matter to the Secretary of State.

**Note**
See the two sets of rules referred to in the note to s. 21(2).

**7(4) [Extra information, etc.]** The Secretary of State or the official receiver may require the liquidator, administrator or administrative receiver of a company, or the former liquidator, administrator or administrative receiver of a company—

(a) to furnish him with such information with respect to any person's conduct as a director of the company, and

(b) to produce and permit inspection of such books, papers and other records relevant to that person's conduct as such a director,

as the Secretary of State or the official receiver may reasonably require for the purpose of determining whether to exercise, or of exercising, any function of his under this section.

**Important CCH Note for s. 6, 7**
A further subsection inserted by Building Societies Act 1986, s. 120 and Sch. 18, para. 17(3) as from 1 January 1987 (see SI 1986 No. 1560 (C. 56)) in regard to the former provision, Insolvency Act 1985, s. 12 — the insertion was intended to be s. 12(10). The new subsection should appear in the current provisions (s. 6, 7) as a result of Sch. 3, para. 6 of this Act and Interpretation Act 1978, s. 17(2)(a). The new subsection, if inserted here as s. 7(5) and revised to take into account other relevant current provisions, would read as follows:

"**7(5)** In this section and in sections 6, 9, 10 and 15 and in sections 212 and 214 to 217 of the Insolvency Act, a reference to a company or to a director (but not a shadow director) of a company includes a reference to a building society within the meaning of the Building Societies Act 1986 or to a director of a building society."

Note that the first words of the subsection set out in the Building Societies Act read "(10) In this section and in sections 14 to 19 . . ."

## Section 8 Disqualification after investigation of company

**8(1) [Application by Secretary of State]** If it appears to the Secretary of State from a report made by inspectors under section 437 of the Companies Act or section 94 or 177 of the Financial Services Act 1986, or from information or documents obtained under section 447 or 448 of the Companies Act or section 105 of the Financial Services Act 1986 or section 2 of the Criminal Justice Act 1987 or section 52 of the Criminal Justice (Scotland) Act 1987, that it is expedient in the public interest that a disqualification order should be made against any person who is or has been a director or shadow director of any company, he may apply to the court for such an order to be made against that person.

**History**
In s. 8(1) the words "or section 94 or 177 of the Financial Services Act 1986" inserted by Financial Services Act 1986, s. 198(2)(a) as from 15 November 1986 (see SI 1986 No. 1940 (C. 69)) and the words "the Companies Act or section 105 of the Financial Services Act 1986" substituted for the former words "that Act" by Financial Services Act 1986, s. 198(2)(b) as from 18 December 1986 (see SI 1986 No. 2246 (C. 88)). In addition the words "or section 52 of the Criminal Justice (Scotland) Act 1987" inserted by Criminal Justice (Scotland) Act 1987, s. 55(b) as from 1 January 1988 (see SI 1987 No. 2119 (C. 62) (S. 143)). Also inserted are the words "or section 2 of the Criminal Justice Act 1987" after the words "the Financial Services Act 1986" in the second place where they occur, by Criminal Justice Act 1988, s. 145(b) as from 12 October 1988 (see SI 1988 No. 1676 (C. 60)).

**8(2) [Court's power]** The court may make a disqualification order against a person where, on an application under this section, it is satisfied that his conduct in relation to the company makes him unfit to be concerned in the management of a company.

**8(3) ["The court"]** In this section **"the court"** means the High Court or, in Scotland, the Court of Session.

**8(4) [Maximum period]** The maximum period of disqualification under this section is 15 years.

## Section 9 Matters for determining unfitness of directors

**9(1) [Matters in Sch. 1]** Where it falls to a court to determine whether a person's conduct as a director or shadow director of any particular company or companies makes him unfit to be concerned in the management of a company, the court shall, as respects his conduct as a director of that company or, as the case may be, each of those companies, have regard in particular—

(a) to the matters mentioned in Part I of Schedule 1 to this Act, and

(b) where the company has become insolvent, to the matters mentioned in Part II of that Schedule;

and references in that Schedule to the director and the company are to be read accordingly.

**9(2) [Application of s. 6(2)]** Section 6(2) applies for the purposes of this section and Schedule 1 as it applies for the purposes of sections 6 and 7.

**9(3) [Interpretation of Sch. 1]** Subject to the next subsection, any reference in Schedule 1 to an enactment contained in the Companies Act or the Insolvency Act includes, in relation to any time before the coming into force of that enactment, the corresponding enactment in force at that time.

**9(4) [Modification of Sch. 1]** The Secretary of State may by order modify any of the provisions of Schedule 1; and such an order may contain such transitional provisions as may appear to the Secretary of State necessary or expedient.

**9(5) [Power exercisable by statutory instrument, etc.]** The power to make orders under this section is exercisable by statutory instrument subject to annulment in pursuance of a resolution of either House of Parliament.

OTHER CASES OF DISQUALIFICATION

## Section 10 Participation in wrongful trading

**10(1) [Court's power]** Where the court makes a declaration under section 213 or 214 of the Insolvency Act that a person is liable to make a contribution to a company's assets, then, whether or not an application for such an order is made by any person, the court may, if it thinks fit, also make a disqualification order against the person to whom the declaration relates.

**10(2) [Maximum period]** The maximum period of disqualification under this section is 15 years.

## Section 11 Undischarged bankrupts

**11(1) [Offence]** It is an offence for a person who is an undischarged bankrupt to act as director of, or directly or indirectly to take part in or be concerned in the promotion, formation or management of, a company, except with the leave of the court.

**11(2) [“The court”]** **“The court”** for this purpose is the court by which the person was adjudged bankrupt or, in Scotland, sequestration of his estates was awarded.

**11(3) [Requirements for leave of court]** In England and Wales, the leave of the court shall not be given unless notice of intention to apply for it has been served on the official receiver; and it is the latter's duty, if he is of opinion that it is contrary to the public interest that the application should be granted, to attend on the hearing of the application and oppose it.

## Section 12 Failure to pay under county court administration order

**12(1) [Effect of s. 12(2)]** The following has effect where a court under section 429 of the Insolvency Act revokes an administration order under Part VI of the County Courts Act 1984.

**12(2) [Restriction on person]** A person to whom that section applies by virtue of the order under section 429(2)(b) shall not, except with the leave of the court which made the order, act as director or liquidator of, or directly or indirectly take part or be concerned in the promotion, formation or management of, a company.

CONSEQUENCES OF CONTRAVENTION

## Section 13 Criminal penalties

**13** If a person acts in contravention of a disqualification order or of section 12(2), or is guilty of an offence under section 11, he is liable—

(a) on conviction on indictment, to imprisonment for not more than 2 years or a fine or both; and

(b) on summary conviction, to imprisonment for not more than 6 months or a fine not exceeding the statutory maximum, or both.

## Section 14 Offences by body corporate

**14(1) [Offence re officer]** Where a body corporate is guilty of an offence of acting in contravention of a disqualification order, and it is proved that the offence occurred with the consent or connivance of, or was attributable to any neglect on the part of any director, manager, secretary or other similar officer of the body corporate, or any person who was purporting to act in any such capacity he, as well as the body corporate, is guilty of the offence and liable to be proceeded against and punished accordingly.

**14(2) [Where managers are members]** Where the affairs of a body corporate are managed by its members, subsection (1) applies in relation to the acts and defaults of a member in connection with his functions of management as if he were a director of the body corporate.

## Section 15 Personal liability for company's debts where person acts while disqualified

**15(1) [Personal liability]** A person is personally responsible for all the relevant debts of a company if at any time—

(a) in contravention of a disqualification order or of section 11 of this Act he is involved in the management of the company, or

(b) as a person who is involved in the management of the company, he acts or is willing to act on instructions given without the leave of the court by a person whom he knows at that time to be the subject of a disqualification order or to be an undischarged bankrupt.

**15(2) [Joint and several liability]** Where a person is personally responsible under this section for the relevant debts of a company, he is jointly and severally liable in respect of those debts with the company and any other person who, whether under this section or otherwise, is so liable.

**15(3) [Relevant debts of company]** For the purposes of this section the relevant debts of a company are—

(a) in relation to a person who is personally responsible under paragraph (a) of subsection (1), such debts and other liabilities of the company as are incurred at a time when that person was involved in the management of the company, and

(b) in relation to a person who is personally responsible under paragraph (b) of that subsection, such debts and other liabilities of the company as are incurred at a time when that person was acting or was willing to act on instructions given as mentioned in that paragraph.

**15(4) [Person involved in management]** For the purposes of this section, a person is involved in the management of a company if he is a director of the company or if he is concerned, whether directly or indirectly, or takes part, in the management of the company.

**15(5) [Interpretation]** For the purposes of this section a person who, as a person involved in the management of a company, has at any time acted on instructions given without the leave of the court by a person whom he knew at that time to be the subject of a disqualification order or to be an undischarged bankrupt is presumed, unless the contrary is shown, to have been willing at any time thereafter to act on any instructions given by that person.

SUPPLEMENTARY PROVISIONS

## Section 16 Application for disqualification order

**16(1) [Notice, appearance, etc.]** A person intending to apply for the making of a disqualification order by the court having jurisdiction to wind up a company shall give not less than 10 days' notice of his intention to the person against whom the order is sought; and on the hearing of the application the last-mentioned person may appear and himself give evidence or call witnesses.

**16(2) [Applicants]** An application to a court with jurisdiction to wind up companies for the making against any person of a disqualification order under any of sections 2 to 5 may be made by the Secretary of State or the official receiver, or by the liquidator or any past or present member or creditor of any company in relation to which that person has committed or is alleged to have committed an offence or other default.

**16(3) [Appearance, etc. of applicant]** On the hearing of any application under this Act made by the Secretary of State or the official receiver or the liquidator, the applicant shall appear and call the attention of the court to any matters which seem to him to be relevant, and may himself give evidence or call witnesses.

## Section 17 Application for leave under an order

**17(1) [Court]** As regards the court to which application must be made for leave under a disqualification order, the following applies—

(a) where the application is for leave to promote or form a company, it is any court with jurisdiction to wind up companies, and

(b) where the application is for leave to be a liquidator, administrator or director of, or otherwise to take part in the management of a company, or to be a receiver or manager of a company's property, it is any court having jurisdiction to wind up that company.

**17(2) [Appearance, etc. of Secretary of State et al.]** On the hearing of an application for leave made by a person against whom a disqualification order has been made on the application of the Secretary of State, the official receiver or the liquidator, the Secretary of State, official receiver or liquidator shall appear and call the attention of the court to any matters which seem to him to be relevant, and may himself give evidence or call witnesses.

## Section 18 Register of disqualification orders

**18(1) [Regulations re furnishing information]** The Secretary of State may make regulations requiring officers of courts to furnish him with such particulars as the regulations may specify of cases in which—

(a) a disqualification order is made, or

(b) any action is taken by a court in consequence of which such an order is varied or ceases to be in force, or

(c) leave is granted by a court for a person subject to such an order to do any thing which otherwise the order prohibits him from doing;

and the regulations may specify the time within which, and the form and manner in which, such particulars are to be furnished.

**Note**
See The Companies (Disqualification Orders) Regulations 1986 (SI 1986 No. 2067).

**18(2) [Register of orders]** The Secretary of State shall, from the particulars so furnished, continue to maintain the register of orders, and of cases in which leave has been granted as mentioned in subsection (1)(c), which was set up by him under section 29 of the Companies Act 1976 and continued under section 301 of the Companies Act 1985.

**18(3) [Deletion of orders no longer in force]** When an order of which entry is made in the register ceases to be in force, the Secretary of State shall delete the entry from the register and all particulars relating to it which have been furnished to him under this section or any previous corresponding provision.

**18(4) [Inspection of register]** The register shall be open to inspection on payment of such fee as may be specified by the Secretary of State in regulations.

**18(5) [Regulations by statutory instrument, etc.]** Regulations under this section shall be made by statutory instrument subject to annulment in pursuance of a resolution of either House of Parliament.

## Section 19 Special savings from repealed enactments

**19** Schedule 2 to this Act has effect—

(a) in connection with certain transitional cases arising under sections 93 and 94 of the Companies Act 1981, so as to limit the power to make a disqualification order, or to restrict the duration of an order, by reference to events occurring or things done before those sections came into force,

(b) to preserve orders made under section 28 of the Companies Act 1976 (repealed by the Act of 1981), and

(c) to preclude any applications for a disqualification order under section 6 or 8, where the relevant company went into liquidation before 28th April 1986.

MISCELLANEOUS AND GENERAL

## Section 20 Admissibility in evidence of statements

**20** In any proceedings (whether or not under this Act), any statement made in pursuance of a requirement imposed by or under sections 6 to 10, 15 or 19(c) of, or Schedule 1 to, this Act, or by or under rules made for the purposes of this Act under the Insolvency Act, may be used in evidence against any person making or concurring in making the statement.

## Section 21 Interaction with Insolvency Act

**21(1) [Reference to official receiver]** References in this Act to the official receiver, in relation to the winding up of a company or the bankruptcy of an individual, are to any person who, by virtue of section 399 of the Insolvency Act, is authorised to act as the official receiver in relation to that winding up or bankruptcy; and, in accordance with section 401(2) of that Act, references in this Act to an official receiver includes a person appointed as his deputy.

**21(2) [Pt. I to VII of IA]** Sections 6 to 10, 15, 19(c) and 20 of, and Schedule 1 to, this Act are deemed included in Parts I to VII of the Insolvency Act for the purposes of the following sections of that Act—

section 411 (power to make insolvency rules);

section 414 (fees orders);

section 420 (orders extending provisions about insolvent companies to insolvent partnerships);

section 422 (modification of such provisions in their application to recognised banks); and

section 431 (summary proceedings).

**Note**

In regard to the entry for s. 411 see The Insolvent Companies (Reports on Conduct of Directors) No. 2 Rules

1986 (SI 1986 No. 2134) and The Insolvent Companies (Reports on Conduct of Directors) (No. 2) (Scotland) Rules 1986 (SI 1986 No. 1916 (S. 140)).

In regard to the entry for s. 420 see The Insolvent Partnerships Order 1986 (SI No. 2142).

**21(3) [Application of IA, s. 434]** Section 434 of that Act (Crown application) applies to sections 6 to 10, 15, 19(c) and 20 of, and Schedule 1 to, this Act as it does to the provisions of that Act which are there mentioned.

## Section 22 Interpretation

**22(1) [Effect]** This section has effect with respect to the meaning of expressions used in this Act, and applies unless the context otherwise requires.

**22(2) ["Company"]** The expression **"company"**—

(a) in section 11, includes an unregistered company, a building society (within the meaning of the Building Societies Act 1986) and a company incorporated outside Great Britain which has an established place of business in Great Britain, and

(b) elsewhere, includes any company which may be wound up under Part V of the Insolvency Act and a building society (within the meaning of the Building Societies Act 1986).

**History**

In s. 22(2) the words ", a building society (within the meaning of the Building Societies Act 1986)" in para. (a) and the words "and a building society (within the meaning of the Building Societies Act 1986)" in para. (b) inserted by Building Societies Act 1986, s. 120 and Sch. 18, para. 16 as from 1 January 1987 (see SI 1986 No. 1560 (C. 56)) in regard to the former provisions, s. 302(4) and s. 295(3) respectively of Companies Act 1985. These words included in the current provisions as result of Sch. 3, para. 6 of this Act and of Interpretation Act 1978, s. 17(2)(a).

**22(3) [Application of IA, ss. 247, 251]** Section 247 in Part VII of the Insolvency Act (interpretation for the first Group of Parts of that Act) applies as regards references to a company's insolvency and to its going into liquidation; and **"administrative receiver"** has the meaning given by section 251 of that Act.

**22(4) ["Director"]** **"Director"** includes any person occupying the position of director, by whatever name called, and in sections 6 to 9 includes a shadow director.

**22(5) ["Shadow director"]** **"Shadow director"**, in relation to a company, means a person in accordance with whose directions or instructions the directors of the company are accustomed to act (but so that a person is not deemed a shadow director by reason only that the directors act on advice given by him in a professional capacity).

**22(6) [Application of CA, ss. 740, 744]** Section 740 of the Companies Act applies as regards the meaning of **"body corporate"**; and **"officer"** has the meaning given by section 744 of that Act.

**22(7) [References to legislation]** In references to legislation other than this Act—

**"the Companies Act"** means the Companies Act 1985;

**"the Companies Acts"** has the meaning given by section 744 of that Act; and

**"the Insolvency Act"** means the Insolvency Act 1986;

and in sections 3(1) and 5(1) of this Act **"the companies legislation"** means the

Companies Acts (except the Insider Dealing Act), Parts I to VII of the Insolvency Act and, in Part XV of that Act, sections 411, 413, 414, 416 and 417.

**22(8) [References to former legislation]** Any reference to provisions, or a particular provision, of the Companies Acts or the Insolvency Act includes the corresponding provisions or provision of the former Companies Acts (as defined by section 735(1)(c) of the Companies Act, but including also that Act itself) or, as the case may be, the Insolvency Act 1985.

**22(9) [Application of CA, Pt. XXVI]** Any expression for whose interpretation provision is made by Part XXVI of the Companies Act (and not by subsections (3) to (8) above) is to be construed in accordance with that provision.

## Section 23 Transitional provisions, savings, repeals

**23(1) [Sch. 3]** The transitional provisions and savings in Schedule 3 to this Act have effect, and are without prejudice to anything in the Interpretation Act 1978 with regard to the effect of repeals.

**23(2) [Sch. 4]** The enactments specified in the second column of Schedule 4 to this Act are repealed to the extent specified in the third column of that Schedule.

## Section 24 Extent

**24(1) [England, Wales, Scotland]** This Act extends to England and Wales and to Scotland.

**24(2) [Northern Ireland]** Nothing in this Act extends to Northern Ireland.

## Section 25 Commencement

**25** This Act comes into force simultaneously with the Insolvency Act 1986.

**Note**

The relevant date is 29 December 1986 — see Insolvency Act 1986, s. 443 and SI 1986 No. 1924 (C. 71).

## Section 26 Citation

**26** This Act may be cited as the Company Directors Disqualification Act 1986.

# SCHEDULES

## Schedule 1 — Matters for Determining Unfitness of Directors

Section 9

### Part I — Matters Applicable in all Cases

**1** Any misfeasance or breach of any fiduciary or other duty by the director in relation to the company.

**2** Any misapplication or retention by the director of, or any conduct by the director giving rise to an obligation to account for, any money or other property of the company.

**3** The extent of the director's responsibility for the company entering into any transaction liable to be set aside under Part XVI of the Insolvency Act (provisions against debt avoidance).

**4** The extent of the director's responsibility for any failure by the company to comply with any of the following provisions of the Companies Act, namely—

(a) section 221 (companies to keep accounting records);

(b) section 222 (where and for how long records to be kept);

(c) section 288 (register of directors and secretaries);

(d) section 352 (obligation to keep and enter up register of members);

(e) section 353 (location of register of members);

(f) section 363 and 364 (company's duty to make annual return);

(g) section 365 (time for completion of annual return); and

(h) sections 399 and 415 (company's duty to register charges it creates).

**5** The extent of the director's responsibility for any failure by the directors of the company to comply with section 227 (directors' duty to prepare annual accounts) or section 238 (signing of balance sheet and documents to be annexed) of the Companies Act.

**5A** In the application of this Schedule to the directors of a building society, references to sections of the Insolvency Act or of the Companies Act other than sections which apply to building societies or their directors in any event, whether by virtue of the Insolvency Act or of the Building Societies Act 1986, shall be construed as references to the corresponding provisions (if any) of the Building Societies Act 1986.

**History**
Para. 5A inserted by Building Societies Act 1986, s. 120 and Sch. 18, para. 17(4) as from 1 January 1987 (see SI 1986 No. 1560 (C. 56)) in regard to the former Sch. 2 of Insolvency Act 1985. This paragraph included in the current schedule as result of Sch. 3, para. 6 of this Act and of Interpretation Act 1978, s. 17(2)(a). Reference to "This Act or of the 1985 Act" and to "this Act" replaced by CCH with references to "the Insolvency Act or of the Companies Act" and to "the Insolvency Act".

## Part II — Matters Applicable Where Company Has Become Insolvent

**6** The extent of the director's responsibility for the causes of the company becoming insolvent.

**7** The extent of the director's responsibility for any failure by the company to supply any goods or services which have been paid for (in whole or in part).

**8** The extent of the director's responsibility for the company entering into any transaction or giving any preference, being a transaction or preference—

(a) liable to be set aside under section 127 or sections 238 to 240 of the Insolvency Act, or

(b) challengeable under section 242 or 243 of that Act or under any rule of law in Scotland.

**9** The extent of the director's responsibility for any failure by the directors of the company to comply with section 98 of the Insolvency Act (duty to call creditors' meeting in creditors' voluntary winding up).

**10** Any failure by the director to comply with any obligation imposed on him by or under any of the following provisions of the Insolvency Act—

(a) section 22 (company's statement of affairs in administration);

(b) section 47 (statement of affairs to administrative receiver);

(c) section 66 (statement of affairs in Scottish receivership);

(d) section 99 (directors' duty to attend meeting; statement of affairs in creditors' voluntary winding up);

(e) section 131 (statement of affairs in winding up by the court);

(f) section 234 (duty of any one with company property to deliver it up);

(g) section 235 (duty to co-operate with liquidator, etc.).

## Schedule 2 — Savings from Companies Act 1981 ss. 93, 94, and Insolvency Act 1985 Schedule 9

Section 19

**1** Sections 2 and 4(1)(b) do not apply in relation to anything done before 15th June 1982 by a person in his capacity as liquidator of a company or as receiver or manager of a company's property.

**2** Subject to paragraph 1—

(a) section 2 applies in a case where a person is convicted on indictment of an offence which he committed (and, in the case of a continuing offence, has ceased to commit) before 15th June 1982; but in such a case a disqualification order under that section shall not be made for a period in excess of 5 years;

(b) that section does not apply in a case where a person is convicted summarily—

(i) in England and Wales, if he had consented so to be tried before that date, or

(ii) in Scotland, if the summary proceedings commenced before that date.

**3** Subject to paragraph 1, section 4 applies in relation to an offence committed or other thing done before 15th June 1982; but a disqualification order made on the grounds of such an offence or other thing done shall not be made for a period in excess of 5 years.

**4** The powers of a court under section 5 are not exercisable in a case where a person is convicted of an offence which he committed (and, in the case of a continuing offence, had ceased to commit) before 15th June 1982.

**5** For purposes of section 3(1) and section 5, no account is to be taken of any offence which was committed, or any default order which was made, before 1st June 1977.

**6** An order made under section 28 of the Companies Act 1976 has effect as if made under section 3 of this Act; and an application made before 15th June 1982 for such an order is to be treated as an application for an order under the section last mentioned.

**7** Where—

(a) an application is made for a disqualification order under section 6 of this Act by virtue of paragraph (a) of subsection (2) of that section, and

(b) the company in question went into liquidation before 28th April 1986 (the coming into force of the provision replaced by section 6).

the court shall not make an order under that section unless it could have made a disqualification order under section 300 of the Companies Act as it had effect immediately before the date specified in sub-paragraph (b) above.

**8** An application shall not be made under section 8 of this Act in relation to a report made or information or documents obtained before 28th April 1986.

## Schedule 3 — Transitional Provisions and Savings

Section 23(1)

**1** In this Schedule, **"the former enactments"** means so much of the Companies Act, and so much of the Insolvency Act, as is repealed and replaced by this Act; and **"the appointed day"** means the day on which this Act comes into force.

**2** So far as anything done or treated as done under or for the purposes of any provision of the former enactments could have been done under or for the purposes of the corresponding provision of this Act, it is not invalidated by the repeal of that provision but has effect as if done under or for the purposes of the corresponding provision; and any order, regulation, rule or other instrument made or having effect under any provision of the former enactments shall, insofar as its effect is preserved by this paragraph, be treated for all purposes as made and having effect under the corresponding provision.

**3** Where any period of time specified in a provision of the former enactments is currently immediately before the appointed day, this Act has effect as if the corresponding provision had been in force when the period began to run; and (without prejudice to the foregoing) any period of time so specified and current is deemed for the purposes of this Act—

(a) to run from the date or event from which it was running immediately before the appointed day, and

(b) to expire (subject to any provision of this Act for its extension) whenever it would have expired if this Act had not been passed;

and any rights, priorities, liabilities, reliefs, obligations, requirements, powers, duties or exemptions dependent on the beginning, duration or end of such a period as above mentioned shall be under this Act as they were or would have been under the former enactments.

**4** Where in any provision of this Act there is a reference to another such provision, and the first-mentioned provision operates, or is capable of operating, in relation to things done or omitted, or events occurring or not occurring, in the past (including in particular past acts of compliance with any enactment, failures of compliance, contraventions, offences and convictions of offences) the reference to the other provision is to be read as including a reference to the corresponding provision of the former enactments.

**5** Offences committed before the appointed day under any provision of the former enactments may, notwithstanding any repeal by this Act, be prosecuted and punished after that day as if this Act had not passed.

**6** A reference in any enactment, instrument or document (whether express or implied, and in whatever phraseology) to a provision of the former enactments (including the corresponding provision of any yet earlier enactment) is to be read, where necessary to retain for the enactment, instrument or document the same force and effect as it would have had but for the passing of this Act, as, or as including, a reference to the corresponding provision by which it is replaced in this Act.

## Schedule 4 — Repeals

Section 23(2)

| Chapter | Short title | Extent of repeal |
|---|---|---|
| 1985 c. 6. | The Companies Act 1985. | Sections 295 to 299.<br>Section 301.<br>Section 302.<br>Schedule 12.<br>In Schedule 24, the entries relating to sections 295(7) and 302(1). |
| 1985 c. 65. | The Insolvency Act 1985. | Sections 12 to 14.<br>Section 16.<br>Section 18.<br>Section 108(2).<br>Schedule 2.<br>In Schedule 6, paragraphs 1, 2, 7 and 14.<br>In Schedule 9, paragraphs 2 and 3. |

## TABLE OF DERIVATIONS

*Note:* The following abbreviations are used in this Table:—

"CA" = The Companies Act 1985 (c. 6).
"IA" = The Insolvency Act 1985 (c. 65).

| Provision | Derivation |
|---|---|
| 1 | CA sec. 295(1), (2), (4); IA Sch. 6 para. 1(1)–(3). |
| 2 | CA ss. 295(2), 296. |
| 3 | CA ss. 295(2), 297. |
| 4 | CA ss. 295(2), 298. |
| 5 | CA ss. 295(2), 299. |
| 6 | CA sec. 295(2); IA ss. 12(1), (2), (7)–(9), 108(2). |
| 7 | IA sec. 12(3)–(6). |
| 8 | CA sec. 295(2); IA ss. 12(9), 13, 108(2). |
| 9 | IA ss. 12(9), 14. |
| 10 | CA sec. 295(2); IA ss. 16, 108(2). |
| 11 | CA sec. 302. |
| 12 | IA sec. 221(2). |
| 13 | CA ss. 295(7), 302(1), Sch. 24. |
| 14 | CA sec. 733(1)–(3); IA Sch. 6 para. 7. |
| 15 | IA sec. 18(1) (part), (2)–(6). |
| 16 | CA sec. 295(6) (part), Sch. 12 paras. 1–3; IA sec. 108(2), Sch. 6 para. 1(4). |
| 17 | CA sec. 295(6) (part), Sch. 12 paras. 4, 5; IA sec. 108(2), Sch. 6 paras. 1(4), 14. |
| 18 | CA sec. 301; IA sec. 108(2), Sch. 6 para. 2. |
| 19 | CA sec. 295(6); and see Sch. 2. |
| 20 | IA sec. 231 (part). |
| 21 | IA ss. 106, 107, 108(1), (2), 222(1), 224(2), 227, 229, 234. |
| 22 | IA sec. 108(1)–(4). |
| 23 | — |
| 24 | IA sec. 236(4)(*a*). |
| 25 | — |
| 26 | — |
| Sch. 1 | IA Sch. 2. |
| Sch. 2 | CA Sch. 12 Pt. III; IA Sch. 9 paras. 2, 3. |
| Sch. 3 | — |
| Sch. 4 | — |

# Appendix II: Explanation of Statutory Terms

These notes are for guidance only: for the full meaning of the terms, reference should be made to the detailed provisions of the relevant Act. For other definitions, see the Company Directors Disqualification Act 1986, s. 22.

**Administrative receiver:** a receiver and manager of the whole (or substantially the whole) of a company's property, appointed by or on behalf of the holders of debentures secured by a floating charge (IA 1986, s. 251).

**Administrator:** an insolvency practitioner appointed by the court under IA 1986, s. 8 to manage the affairs of an insolvent or near-insolvent company, in the hope of securing its survival as a going concern or a more advantageous realisation of its assets than would be effected on a winding-up.

**Become insolvent:** see CDDA 1986, s. 6(2), and ¶407 above.

**Gone into insolvent liquidation:** see IA 1986, s. 214(6), and ¶604 above.

**Involved in the management of a company:** see CDDA 1986, s. 15(4) and ¶201 and ¶702 above.

**Office-holder:** see CDDA 1986, s. 7(3).

**Officer:** this term has no precise statutory meaning: the definition in CA 1985, s. 744 (which also applies to CDDA 1986 and IA 1986) merely states that '"officer" *includes* a director, manager or secretary'. Where a liquidator, administrator or receiver is intended to be covered by a statutory provision, this is usually made clear in the relevant section, and it is reasonable to infer that, where this is not the case, such an office-holder will not be an 'officer'. (An administrator, a receiver and manager and an administrative receiver might, however, be regarded as being a 'manager', in that some of his functions are managerial.) An auditor has been held to be an 'officer' for the purposes of the precursors to IA 1986, s. 212, but the point is not free from doubt. Bankers, solicitors and other professional advisers are not, as such, 'officers' of the company. The greatest uncertainty surrounds the term 'manager', which the statutory definition refers to. In *Re a Company No. 00996 of 1979* [1980] Ch. 138, at p. 144, Shaw LJ said:

> 'The expression "manager" should not be too narrowly construed. It is not to be equated with a managing or other director or a general manager . . . [Any] person who in the affairs of the company exercises a supervisory control which reflects the general policy of the company or which is related to the general administration of the company is in the sphere of management. He need not be a member of the board of directors. He need not be subject to specific instructions from the board.'

**Shadow director:** a person in accordance with whose directions or instructions the directors of a company are accustomed to act (excluding a person who gives advice in a professional capacity): CA 1985, s. 741(2) and CDDA 1986, s. 22(5); see ¶109 above.

# Appendix III: Reported Cases

Reported cases on director disqualification include the following:

*R* v *Austen* (1985) 1 BCC 99,528; (1985) 7 Cr App R (S) 214 [CA 1948, s. 188 (CDDA 1986, s. 2)]

Seven companies; director convicted on nine counts of dishonesty involving £300,000. Three years' imprisonment; disqualification order made for ten years.

*Re Dawson Print Group Ltd & Anor* (1987) 3 BCC 322 [CA 1985, s. 300 (CDDA 1986, s. 6)]

Two companies; net deficit £121,000; mismanagement but not reckless; 'some bad luck'; misuse of Crown debts; third business thriving: no disqualification order made.

*Re Stanford Services Ltd & Ors* (1987) 3 BCC 326 [CA 1985, s. 300 (CDDA 1986, s. 6)]

Three companies; net deficit £559,000; undercapitalisation; misuse of Crown debts; failure to file returns; continuing to trade and to draw remuneration when ought to have been aware of imminent insolvency: disqualification order made for two years.

*R* v *Churchill Hotel (Plymouth) Ltd & Ors* (1988) 4 BCC 112 [CA 1985, s. 300 (CDDA 1986, s. 6)]

Four companies; net deficit £787,000; undercapitalisation; misuse of Crown debts; failure to file returns; companies traded unprofitably throughout their existence; no dishonesty; other companies employing 80 people being responsibly run: borderline case but no disqualification order made.
[Note: the court exercised a discretion which is no longer available under CDDA 1986, s. 6.]

*Re Bath Glass Ltd* (1988) 4 BCC 130 [CDDA 1986, s. 6]

One company; net deficit £128,000; misuse of Crown debts; failure to file accounts on one occasion; had continued to trade and to draw remuneration when knew or ought to have been aware of imminent insolvency; conduct imprudent but no dishonesty; directors had acted on professional advice and with budgets and profit forecasts: not 'unfit'; no disqualification order made.

*R* v *Georgiou* (1988) 4 BCC 322; (1988) 87 Cr App R 207 [CDDA 1986, s. 2]

Defendant was convicted of the offence of carrying on an insurance business without authorisation through a company contrary to the Insurance Companies Act 1982. Sentenced to six months' imprisonment and disqualification order made for five years.

*Re Lo-Line Electric Motors Ltd & Ors* [1988] Ch. 477; (1988) 4 BCC 415 [CA 1985, s. 300 (CDDA 1986, s. 6)]

Four companies; net deficit £874,000; misuse of Crown debts; failure to file returns; continuing to trade when knew or ought to have been aware of imminent insolvency; not 'consciously dishonest': disqualification order made for three years.

*Re Rolus Properties Ltd & Anor* (1988) 4 BCC 446 [IA 1976, s. 9 (see now CDDA 1986, ss. 6–9]

Two companies; net deficit £100,000; failure to keep books or prepare accounts, or have them audited; failure to file returns; incompetent rather than dishonest: disqualification order made for two years (four to six years would have been appropriate but for the fact that defendant had engaged a chartered secretary to handle paperwork).

*Re Western Welsh International System Buildings Ltd & Ors* (1988) 4 BCC 449 [CA 1985, s. 300 (CDDA 1986, s. 6)]

Three companies; net deficit not stated; misuse of Crown debts; failure to keep proper books or accounts; failure to file returns; continuing to trade when knew or ought to have been aware of imminent insolvency; continuing to accept customers' prepayments when financially unable to fulfil orders: disqualification orders made for five years.

*Re D. J. Matthews (Joinery Design) Ltd & Anor* (1988) 4 BCC 513 [CA 1985, s. 300 (CDDA 1986, s. 6)]

Two companies; net deficit £154,000; undercapitalisation; misuse of Crown debts; failure to keep proper accounts; failure to file returns; continuing to trade when knew or ought to have been aware of imminent insolvency; 'irresponsible and incompetent management'; no personal dishonesty; new business being properly run: disqualification order made for three years.

*Re McNulty's Interchange Ltd & Anor* (1988) 4 BCC 533 [CA 1985, s. 300 (CDDA 1986, s. 6)]

Two companies; net deficit £459,000; first company had traded profitably but experienced downturn; professional advice taken; no impropriety; second company had been allowed to continue to incur expense and debts after business had been sold: disqualification order made for 18 months.

*Re Douglas Construction Services Ltd & Anor* (1988) 4 BCC 553 [CA 1985, s. 300 (CDDA 1986, s. 6)]

Two companies; net deficit £542,000; no undercapitalisation; non-payment of Crown debts; mismanagement but no irresponsibility or incompetence; accounts properly kept by qualified finance director; professional advice taken: no disqualification order made.

*Re J. & B. Lynch (Builders) Ltd* [1988] BCLC 376 [CA 1985, s. 300 (CDDA 1986, s. 6)]

Four companies; net deficit £93,000; non-payment of Crown debts; inadequate records kept; no returns or accounts filed; continued to trade when knew company insolvent; issued numerous cheques which were dishonoured; disqualification order made for three years.

## Selected extracts from the judgments in reported cases

(1) *Re Bath Glass Ltd* (1988) 4 BCC 130 (Peter Gibson J):

'. . . Take a case of wrongful trading. In proceedings brought by the liquidator under s. 214 a director may be held liable under that section because for a short time before the commencement of the liquidation the director allowed the company so to trade and a small contribution might be ordered under that section. In those circumstances it is not surprising that no minimum period of disqualification is provided. In contrast the test in s. 6 is quite different: there is no single specified offence that is the condition to be satisfied for the court to make a disqualification order. What the court must have regard to is the director's conduct; that is a term of great generality and I do not doubt that it was deliberately so chosen. The court must be satisfied that the conduct in question is sufficiently serious to lead it to the conclusion that the director is unfit and that is emphasised by the mandatory disqualification for at least two years to be imposed by the court if that conclusion is reached.

To reach a finding of unfitness the court must be satisfied that the director has been guilty of a serious failure or serious failures, whether deliberately or through incompetence, to perform those duties of directors which are attendant on the privilege of trading through companies with limited liability. Any misconduct of the respondent qua director may be relevant, even if it does not fall within a specific section of the Companies Acts or the Insolvency Act. For example, the authorities under the previous disqualification legislation show that the court will regard as relevant misconduct the fact that a director, as he knew or ought to have known, caused a company to trade at the expense and jeopardy of moneys which the company has received, for instance in the form of VAT, from customers or which has been deducted from the emoluments of employees in the form of PAYE tax and National Insurance contributions and for which he ought to have accounted to the Crown on a regular basis. The director ought not to allow the company to use such moneys to finance the company's trade (see *Re Stanford Services Ltd. & Ors.* (1987) 3 BCC 326, at p. 334). Even if such conduct does not amount to wrongful trading within s. 214, in my judgment it would still be conduct amounting to misconduct and so relevant to s. 6. . . .'

(2) *Re Lo-Line Electric Motors Ltd & Ors* (1988) 4 BCC 415 (Browne-Wilkinson V.-C.):

'. . . *The general approach*

What is the proper approach to deciding whether someone is unfit to be a director? The approach adopted in all the cases to which I have been referrred is broadly the same. The primary purpose of the section is not to punish the individual but to protect the public against the future conduct of companies by persons whose past records as directors of insolvent companies have shown them to be a danger to creditors and others. Therefore, the power is not fundamentally penal. But if the power to disqualify is exercised, disqualification does involve a substantial interference with the freedom of the individual. It follows that the rights of the individual must be fully protected. Ordinary commercial misjudgment is in itself not sufficient to justify disqualification. In the normal case, the conduct complained of must display a lack of commercial probity although I have no doubt that in an extreme case of gross negligence or total incompetence disqualification could be appropriate.

*Natural justice*

Since the making of a disqualification order involves penal consequences for the director, it is necessary that he should know the substance of the charges that he has to meet. The practice of the official receiver is to summarise the allegations of misconduct on which he is going to rely in the affidavit in support. This procedure is plainly both desirable and necessary. . . .

I am not differing from the views expressed by *Peter Gibson* J. in *Re Churchill Hotel (Plymouth) Ltd. & Ors.* (1988) 4 BCC 112 where he held (at pp. 115–116) that the court should not refuse to look at an allegation just because the official receiver had not given prior notice of it provided that, by adjournment to file evidence or otherwise, there would be no injustice to the director. But the requirements of natural justice must depend on the circumstances of each case and in my judgment a fundamental change of case from one alleging commercial dishonesty to one alleging crass commercial misjudgment is a change of a nature which requires wholly different evidence and prior notice should have been given.

*Conflicts of evidence*

In the present case there are many factual issues on which the evidence given by Mr. Browning in his affidavits directly contradicts allegations made against him by the official receiver. Yet he has not been cross-examined. In my judgment proceedings for disqualification are no different from any other court proceedings: it is not possible for the court to disbelieve evidence given on oath in the absence of cross-examination of the witness. I therefore proceed on the footing that Mr. Browning's evidence is correct.

*Crown debts*

The debts owed by the companies included substantial Crown debts i.e. sums for which the company was liable to the Inland Revenue or Customs and Excise in respect of PAYE, National Insurance and VAT. . . .

Although the Crown debts are not strictly trust moneys, the failure to pay them over does not only prejudice the Crown, as creditor, but in the case of PAYE and National Insurance may also have a prejudicial effect on the company's employees. The use of moneys obtained by compulsory deductions from wages for the financing of the company's business is to use moneys which morally, if not legally, belong either to the employees or to the Crown without the consent of either. I consider the use of the moneys which should have been paid to the Crown to finance continuation of an insolvent company's business more culpable than the failure to pay commercial debts. . . .'

(3) *Re Rolus Properties Ltd & Anor* (1988) 4 BCC 446 (Harman J):

'. . . Mr. Lloyd observed to me – again I think correctly – that the mere fact that the company had been formed and had embarked with small capital upon a speculative venture would not by itself warrant criticism. The grounds for criticism here are that there were no books kept, no statutory returns made, no accounts prepared – a total failure of the paperwork of the company, leading to great difficulties in perceiving exactly what had happened.

The privilege of limited liability is a valuable incentive to encourage entrepreneurs to take on risky ventures without inevitable personal total financial disaster. It is, however, a privilege which must be accorded upon terms and some of the most important terms that Parliament has imposed are that accounts be kept and returns made so that the world can, by referring to those, see what is happening. Thus, a total failure to keep statutory books and to make statutory returns is significant for the public at large and is a matter which amounts to misconduct if not complied with and is a matter of which the court should take account in considering whether a man can properly be allowed to continue to operate as a director of companies, or whether the public at large is to be protected against him on the grounds that he is unfit, not because he is fraudulent but because he is incompetent and unable to comply with the statutory obligations attached to limited liability. In my view that is a correct approach and the jurisdiction does extend and should be exercised in cases where a man has by his conduct revealed that he is wholly unable to comply with the obligations that go with the privilege of limited liability. . . .

It might be thought that two companies, one run for five years during which no accounts of any sort were kept and the other run without any adequate accounts for a shorter period, would show that Mr. Whyte was so hopelessly unfit because, probably, of a lack of understanding of paperwork, as to be somebody who should be kept off the limited company scene for the protection of the public for quite a substantial period. Something of the order of four, or even, under the wider jurisdiction which is not available here, perhaps six years might have been a suitable time to protect the public from his incompetence. But the fact is that there is a substantial mitigating factor here. Mr. Whyte had as his associate a gentleman called Thomas Weighill. Mr. Weighill was the secretary of the company. . . . He was in fact, he says, and Mr. Whyte confirmed, not a director of the company and there is no evidence to the contrary. It is clear that he took no part in the running of the company. However, Mr. Weighill says that he is a chartered secretary and also a commercial accountant working on his own account. Chartered secretaries are gentlemen of considerable qualifications – the Institute of Chartered Secretaries has very severe exams – and anyone who obtains a chartered secretary to assist in the administration of the affairs of a company, large or small, would, in my view, have reasonable grounds for saying that he had taken proper steps to provide the company with an officer who would, by definition above all others, be competent to and should be able to prepare all necessary paperwork. That, indeed, is what chartered secretaries' businesses are primarily about – control of documents, returns, and keeping up with statutory obligations. . . .

In all the circumstances, it seems to me, I must take into account in Mr. Whyte's favour the fact that he had obtained suitable qualified professional assistance to fill what appear to have been Mr. Whyte's own deficiencies, which he thus seems to have recognised in advance and attempted to provide for. That does, to my mind, substantially mitigate the need for protection of the public, which in my belief is the main purpose of this legislation. As I see this legislation it is not primarily punitive; it is primarily for the protection of the public against inadequate, dishonest, or otherwise unfit persons being directors of companies.

On that basis, having started with a view that somewhere around four to six years might have been a suitable time to think of for disqualification, I must, in my judgment, reduce it. I still consider that Mr. Whyte by his conduct has shown that he is not a fit person to be a director of a limited company. I consider that the public ought to be protected from his incompetence and in all the circumstances, trying, in the absence of some material which I would have been grateful to have, to weigh the matter up, I conclude that a period of two years' disqualification from today would be appropriate.'

(4) *Re McNulty's Interchange Ltd & Anor* (1988) 4 BCC 533 (Browne-Wilkinson V.-C.):

'. . . The official receiver says that although Mr. McNulty was not aware that the company was insolvent when it was continuing to trade, he says that he ought to have been aware it was. I reject that allegation on the evidence before me. The evidence is that he was throughout advised by professional financial advisers. To suggest that somebody in those circumstances, who relies on the advisers, is in some way acting improperly, because he does not appreciate that his advisers' advice is wrong, seems to me untenable. It is also said that he was guilty of misconduct in relation to the affairs of Robots in that he failed to pay over PAYE, National Insurance and VAT and retained it in the company. The retention of such Crown debts has certain special features in the ordinary case which in my judgment make it even less acceptable than the failure to pay debts of the company as they fall due. But on the facts of this case the Customs and Excise and the Revenue had apparently agreed to accept payment by instalment and so they were in no sense involuntary creditors; they had agreed to take payment by instalments. The next thing that is said is that he should not have been drawing remuneration out of the company. He was apparently drawing remuneration at the rate of approximately £25,000 a year. Again, there is nothing to suggest that in the light of the information then available that was in any way improper. The truth of the matter was that in the field of advanced technology there was a commercial invention which appeared to have a very good future, in relation to which there was a shortage of capital for research and development and the necessary finance, so it was thought, to cover that shortfall had been raised. It may be that wrong commercial decisions were taken. But I deplore the suggestion that a director who makes what in retrospect appears to be a commercial misjudgment is in some way acting in a manner which is culpable so as to justify disqualification . . .'

(5) *Re Douglas Construction Services Ltd & Anor* (1988) 4 BCC 553 (Harman J):

'. . . It is of vital importance that the court, in operating this very important jurisdiction created by Parliament for the protection of the public against those who use limited liability to abuse the privileges and – to use a colloquialism – rip off the public and cheat, in particular, the authorities, should be careful that it does not so act as to stultify all enterprise. The purpose and the great value of the invention in 1862 of the limited liability company was to enable entrepreneurs to take risks without bankrupting themselves. Down to that date persons had had to trade on their personal liability. Thereafter, if they could get credit, they can trade with the protection of limited liability. That is a great privilege which has caused part of the great expansion of wealth in this country in the last hundred years. It is, of course, a privilege which must be exercised responsibly and cannot be abused and, if abused, the courts must prevent those who abuse it from so doing in the future.

I have, myself, disqualified directors frequently at these sittings for terms of up to ten years, and I have seen enough cases to have some idea of the prevalence of this sort of conduct and to get some idea of the badges of the man who is simply exploiting limited liability in a cynical way with a disregard for proper responsibility or, alternatively, exploiting it because he is so stupid and ignorant that he is quite incapable of appreciating what has happened and thereby causes large losses by, in a sense, incompetence.

In either of those cases the court should protect, in my view, the public from that man further abusing the privileges.

This case seems to me to have none of the badges of that sort. Mr. Genge personally, and his wife, have suffered very substantial losses in these matters. . . .

That is not a case of a man who has taken no risks himself and has not exposed himself in the matter and who has cynically exploited creditors. It is quite true creditors have lost, and it is quite true, I think, that Mr. Genge mismanaged both Douglas in one way and then Hawk in the opposite way, but he mismanaged them in a manner which, in my view, does not make him unfit in any proper sense of that word to be concerned in the future direction of companies. As it seems to me, the history of failure in two companies within five years – which brings Mr. Genge within the reach of these sections – were failures which were commercially understandable, and Mr. Genge acted with proper responsibility.

It is not fair, as Mr. Davis charged him with always saying, "Oh well, I was advised and I am not responsible." He was advised, but he was advised by people on whom any reasonable man could properly expect to be able to rely. He did not evade his responsibilities and shuffle the matter off. He acted, in my view, in a sensible way in getting in a financial man, in the shape of Roberts, who ought to have been able to help him properly, and in the shape of Walton, to ensure that the companies did not fail.

Of course he is responsible as a director. Every director of every company is responsible for all its affairs, and nobody assuming the office of director can say, "I am not responsible for part of the company's affairs", but the question is, has that responsibility been operated in such a way as to render the individual unfit to be a director in the future.

In my view the conduct of Mr. Genge in this case cannot possibly be described as rendering him unfit for the future, and for my part I think that this summons should not have been pursued after the evidence came in showing how the matter was conducted.

I shall refuse to make any order disqualifying Mr. Genge and no question, therefore, arises of my considering his present directorships, whether shadow or legal, other than to say that he has heard what I have said and I hope he will bear in mind that as a director he has responsibilities and he must take care to make sure that all his companies are properly conducted in the future. Beyond that I do not think it right to go.'

(6) *Re Produce Marketing Consortium Ltd* (22 March 1989, to be reported in (1989) 5 BCC 569). A summary is as follows:

The company was incorporated in 1964 and carried on business acting as agents in connection with the importation of fruit from Spain. At first, the business was successful but gradually the number of its directors, its turnover and its profitability diminished. By 1981 D and M were and remained the sole directors until the company went into creditors' voluntary liquidation on 2 October 1987.

A liquidator was appointed on 11 November 1987 and he wrote to the two directors asking for an explanation of the fact that the company had continued to trade whilst insolvent. He then applied to the High Court for an order that the two directors should each contribute £107,946 and such figure for interest and costs or such other sum as the court might think appropriate, to the assets of the company.

That relief was sought under IA 1986, s. 214 which dealt with wrongful trading. The liquidator claimed that from July 1986 the directors should have concluded that there was no reasonable prospect of avoiding insolvent liquidation and ceased trading.

Knox J. said that it was evident that Parliament intended to widen the scope of the legislation under which directors who traded on when the company was insolvent might, in appropriate circumstances, be required to make a contribution to the assets of the company, which in practical terms meant its creditors. Comparing s. 214 with s. 213 (fraudulent trading), the requirement for an intent to defraud and fraudulent purpose was not retained in s. 214 as an essential and with it went the need for actual dishonesty involving real moral blame. (It was never suggested that D and M fell into that category.) Further, the test to be applied by the court in s. 214 was one under which the director in question was to be judged by the standards of what could be expected of a person fulfilling his functions and showing reasonable diligence in doing so (s. 214(4)).

The requirement to have regard to the functions to be carried out by the director in question in relation to the company in question involved having regard to the particular company and its business. It followed that the general knowledge, skill and experience to be attributed to the directors would be much less extensive in a small company in a modest way of business with simple accounting procedures and equipment than it would be in a large company with sophisticated procedures. Nevertheless certain minimum standards were to be assumed to be attained. Notably there was an obligation laid on companies to cause accounting records to be kept which were such as to disclose with reasonable accuracy at any time the financial position of the company (CA 1985, s. 221(1), (2)(*a*)). In addition, directors were required to prepare a profit and loss account for each financial year and a balance sheet at the end of it (s. 227(1), (3)). Directors were also required, in respect of each financial year, to lay before the company in general meeting copies of accounts of the company for that year and to deliver to the Registrar of Companies a copy of those accounts, in the case of a private company, within ten months after the end of the relevant accounting reference period (see s. 241(1), (3) and s. 242(1), (2)).

The knowledge to be imputed in testing whether or not directors knew or ought to have concluded that there was no reasonable prospect of the company avoiding insolvent liquidation was not limited to the documentary material actually available at the given time. That appeared from s. 214(4) which included a reference to facts which a director of the company ought not only to know but those which he ought to ascertain, a word which did not appear in s. 214(2)(*b*). That indicated that there was to be included by way of factual information not only what was actually there but what, given reasonable diligence and an appropriate level of general knowledge, skill and experience, was ascertainable. Therefore, the court would assume for the purposes of applying the test in s. 214(2) that the financial results for the year ended 30 September 1985 were known at the end of July 1986 at least to the extent of the size of the deficiency of assets over liabilities. In all the circumstances, D and M ought to have concluded at the end of July 1986 that there was no reasonable prospect that the company would avoid going into insolvent liquidation.

The next question was whether there was a case under s. 214(3) for saying that after the end of July 1986 D and M took every step with a view to minimising the potential loss to the creditors of the company as, assuming them to have known there was no reasonable prospect of the company avoiding insolvent liquidation, they ought to have taken. That clearly had to be answered 'no' since they went on trading for another year.

Therefore the court's discretion arose under s. 214(1).

In his Lordship's judgment the jurisdiction under s. 214 was primarily compensatory rather than penal. Prima facie the appropriate amount that a director should be declared to be liable to contribute was the amount by which the company's assets could be discerned to have been depleted by the director's conduct which caused the discretion under s. 214(1) to arise. However, Parliament had chosen very wide words of discretion and it would be undesirable to seek to spell out limits on that discretion in the first case to come to judgment under the section.

The fact that there was no fraudulent intent was not of itself a reason for fixing the amount at a nominal or low figure for that would amount to frustrating Parliament's intention in adding s. 214 to s. 213 (which dealt with fraudulent trading) of the 1986 Act. However, it was not right to ignore that fact totally.

This was a case of failure to appreciate what should have been clear rather than a deliberate course of wrongdoing. There were occasions when positive untruths were stated which could not just be treated as unwarranted optimism. A most solemn warning given by the auditor in early February 1987 was effectively ignored. The affairs of the company were conducted during the last seven months of trading in a way which reduced the indebtedness to the bank. The bank was at least substantially secured. The court's jurisdiction needed to be exercised to benefit unsecured creditors. Taking all those circumstances into account, D and M were declared liable under s. 214 to make a total contribution to the company's assets of £75,000. Partly because D was M's senior in every sense, but principally because of the existence of D's guarantee, as between the two of them D should indemnify M as to £50,000 and above that, they should be jointly liable.

# Appendix IV: Forms

## The Insolvent Companies (Reports on Conduct of Directors) No. 2 Rules 1986 (SI 1986 No. 2134)

The liquidator of an insolvent company registered in England and Wales which passes a resolution for voluntary winding-up is required by the Company Directors Disqualification Act 1986, s. 7(3) and the above Rules to make a report to the Secretary of State in Form D1 as set out on p. 92.

Where no report is made within six months from the date of the passing of the resolution for winding-up, an interim return in Form D3 must be furnished (see p. 97).

Similar forms are prescribed to cover the cases where an administrator or an administrative receiver is appointed.

**D1**

COMPANIES IN VOLUNTARY LIQUIDATION

REPORT ON CONDUCT OF DIRECTORS UNDER SECTION 7(3) OF THE COMPANY DIRECTORS DISQUALIFICATION ACT 1986

Before completing this form read the DTI Guidance Notes

| | | Official Use |
|---|---|---|
| Company registered number | ______________________________ | |
| Name of Company | ______________________________ | |
| Registered Office address | ______________________________ | |
| | ______________________________ | |
| Nature of Business | ______________________________ | |
| Trading Names | ______________________________ | |
| Principal place of business | ______________________________ | |
| | ______________________________ | |
| Date of liquidation | ______________________________ | |
| Name of Liquidator | ______________________________ | |
| Office holder number | ______________________________ | |
| Liquidator's address | ______________________________ | |
| | ______________________________ | |
| | ______________________________ | |
| Period covered by report | From: ___________ To: ___________ | |

1. I am the liquidator of the company and it appears to me that the persons listed in the schedule were either directors or shadow directors of the company and **were the only** such directors of the company during the period covered by this report.
2. It further appears to me that the conduct of each of the persons in respect of whom I have marked Y in column 5 in the schedule as a director of the company, either considered in relation to this company alone or taken together with his conduct as a director of any other company, makes him unfit to be concerned in the management of a company. Details of his conduct are provided in Part D1(B) of the report.

**Form D1 continued**

Schedule

| 1<br>Full name and other known names | 2<br>Last known address | 3<br>Mark X if Shadow Director | 4<br>Period as Director<br>From | <br><br>To | 5<br>If you have attached supplementary details please mark with a Y |
|---|---|---|---|---|---|
| | | | | | |

Liquidator's Signature ______________________

Date ___________

Remember to attach forms D1(A) and D1(B)

**Form D1 continued**

**D1(A)**

PART A

FURTHER DETAILS OF THE COMPANY

NAME OF COMPANY

3. Date of incorporation
4. Period of trading From ______________ To ______________
5. Estimated distribution(s) (pence in £) to creditors
   - preferential:
   - unsecured:
6. Summary of statement of affairs

| | £ |
|---|---|
| Gross assets: | ______ |
| Gross liabilities to creditors: | ______ |
| Estimated total deficiency as regards creditors: | ______ |
| Called-up capital: | ______ |

7. Approximate number and value of unsecured creditors distinguishing between

| | No. | £ |
|---|---|---|
| Trade and expense: | ______ | ______ |
| Depositor or consumer pre-paid: | ______ | ______ |
| Connected companies: | ______ | ______ |
| Other: | ______ | ______ |

8. Details of other connected companies with which the company has had any dealings

The above is correct to the best of my knowledge, information and belief.

Liquidator's Signature ______________________

Date ___________

**Form D1 continued**

**D1(B)**

A separate "part B" is to be completed for each Director to be reported upon.

PART B

NAME OF COMPANY

FULLER DETAILS OF THE INDIVIDUAL DIRECTOR SUBJECT TO THIS REPORT

9. Full name of the Director:
10. Date of birth:
11. Occupation, trade or profession:
12. Position(s) held within company:

13. Give details (on such additional pages as necessary) of the conduct of the director, which makes it appear to you that the conditions of Section 6(1) of the Act are satisfied. You should have particular regard to Schedule 1 of the Act.

14. List the remuneration and other benefits during each of the 3 years to the date of liquidation

| Period ended | Remuneration received £ | Remuneration voted £ | Cash expenses £ | Benefits in kind £ |
|---|---|---|---|---|
| | | | | |
| | | | | |
| | | | | |
| | | | | |

15(a) Other companies of which the director is or was during the 3 years to the date of liquidation also a director or shadow director.

| Name of Company Reg. No. | Are you also the Liquidator Administrative Receiver or Administrator of that Company (Y/N) | Mark X here if you are to submit a conduct report in respect of the Company or enter date of report if already submitted |
|---|---|---|
| | | |

(b) Give details of any other companies not listed at Q8 or 15(a) above with which the director may have had an association which you feel may be relevant to the consideration of his conduct.

16. Give brief details of any civil or criminal proceedings in relation to the company taken or likely to be taken against the director.

## Form D1 continued

17. Are there any other matter(s) which you consider the Secretary of State should take into consideration.

The details given in Part D1(B) (comprising ______ pages)
are correct to the best of my knowledge, information and belief.

Liquidator's Signature ________________________

Date ___________

**D3**

COMPANIES IN CREDITORS' VOLUNTARY LIQUIDATION

RETURN OF DIRECTORS UNDER RULE 4 OF THE INSOLVENT COMPANIES

(REPORT ON CONDUCT OF DIRECTORS) NO. 2 RULES 1986

Before completing this form read the DTI Guidance Notes

| | | Official Use |
|---|---|---|
| Company registered number | ______________________ | |
| Name of Company | ______________________ | |
| Registered Office address | ______________________ | |
| | ______________________ | |
| Nature of Business | ______________________ | |
| Trading Names | ______________________ | |
| Principal place of business | ______________________ | |
| | ______________________ | |
| Date of liquidation | ______________________ | |
| Name of Liquidator | ______________________ | |
| Office holder number | ______________________ | |
| Liquidator's address | ______________________ | |
| | ______________________ | |
| | ______________________ | |

Mark with an X the statement which applies

1. (i) I have not submitted a report in this case because:

   (a) ☐ the company has sufficient assets to pay its debts and other liabilities and the expenses of any winding-up

   (b) ☐ as at the date of this return I have not become aware of any matters which would require me to make a report under Section 7(3) of the Act

   (c) ☐ sufficient information is not yet to hand (see below).

   (ii) I have not submitted a report on all of the directors in this case because:

   (d) ☐ as at the date of this return I have not become aware of any matters which would require me to make a report under Section 7(3) of the Act on the remaining directors

   (e) ☐ sufficient information is not yet to hand (see below).

   If you have marked box (c) or box (e) please indicate the likely date when the report if any will be submitted:

   ______________ ______________
   Month Year

## Form D3 continued

2. The persons listed in the schedule were to the best of my knowledge and belief all the persons who were directors or shadow directors of the company during the three years prior to the liquidation.

Schedule

| Full name and other known names | Last known address | Mark X if Shadow Director | Period as Director From | To |
|---|---|---|---|---|
| | | | | |

Liquidator's Signature ______________________

Date ___________

# Case Table

*All references are to paragraph numbers*


**Paragraph**

**A**

Altim Pty Ltd, Re [1968] 2 NSWR 762 . . . 901
Appleyard; R v (1985) 81 Cr App R 319 . . . 402
Arctic Engineering Ltd & Ors, Re [1986] 1 WLR 686; (1985) 1 BCC 99, 563 . . . 202; 403
Austen; R v (1985) 1 BCC 99, 528 . . . 201; 202; 702

**B**

BBK Interiors Ltd, Re (unreported 2 June 1987) . . . 202
Bath Glass Ltd, Re (1988) 4 BCC 130 . . . 412; 413; 416
Blacklager Ltd, Re (unreported 26 February 1987) . . . 202
Blum v O.C.P. Repartition S.A. (1988) 4 BCC 771 . . . 802
British Dental Floss (unofficially reported 13 June 1988) . . . 705

**C**

CCA v Bracht (1989) 7 ACLC 40. . . . . 201
Campbell; R v [1984] BCLC 83 . . . 201; 702
Chandler & Ors v Director of Public Prosecutions [1964] AC 763 . . . 602
Churchill Hotel (Plymouth) Ltd & Ors, Re [1988] 4 BCC 112 . . . 301; 412
City Equitable Fire Insurance Co. Ltd, Re [1925] Ch. 407 . . . 607
Civica Investments Ltd & Ors, Re [1983] BCLC 456 . . . 202
Company No. 005009 of 1987, Re (1988) 4 BCC 424 . . . 109; 605
Corbin; R v (1984) 6 Cr App R (S) 17 . . . 402
Cyona Distributors Ltd, Re [1967] Ch. 889 . . . 505

**D**

Dawson Print Group Ltd & Anor, Re (1987) 3 BCC 322 . . . 412

**Paragraph**

**E**

Eurostem Maritime Ltd & Ors, Re [1987] PCC 190 . . . 109; 413

**F**

Foster; R v (unreported 4 July 1972) . . . 202

**G**

Georgiou; R v (1988) 4 BCC 322 . . . 402
Green and Green; R v (1981) 3 Cr App R (S) 22 . . . 201

**K**

Kayford Ltd, Re [1975] 1 WLR 279 . . . 411

**L**

Lindholst & Co A/S v Fowler & Anor (1988) 4 BCC 776 . . . 802
Liquidator of West Mercia Safetywear Ltd v Dodd & Anor (1988) 4 BCC 30 . . . 609
Lo-Line Electric Motors Ltd & Ors, Re [1988] Ch. 477; (1988) 4 BCC 415 . . . 109; 202; 203; 412; 413; 415; 905

**M**

McQuillan, Re (1989) 5 BCC 137 . . . 901
Magna Alloys and Research Pty Ltd & Ors, Re (unreported 19 September 1975) . . . 201
Majestic Recording Studios Ltd & Ors, Re (1988) 4 BCC 519 . . . 902; 905
Matthews (D.J.) (Joinery Design) Ltd & Anor, Re (1988) 4 BCC 513 . . . 905
Multinational Gas and Petrochemical Co v Multinational Gas and Petrochemical Services Ltd & Ors [1983] Ch. 258 . . . 609

**O**

Oasis Marketing Ltd (unofficially reported 18 June 1988) . . . . . . . . . . 705

**P**

Patrick & Lyon Ltd, Re [1933] Ch. 786 502
Pestroyd Preservations (Ewell) Ltd (unofficially reported 24 May 1988) 705
Produce Marketing Consortium Ltd, Re (1989) 5 BCC 569 . . . . . . . . . . . . . . 615

**R**

R v Appleyard (1985) 81 Cr App R 319 402
— v Austen (1985) 1 BCC 99, 528 . . . 201; 202; 702
— v Campbell [1984] BCLC 83 . . . 201; 702
— v Corbin (1984) 6 Cr App R (S) 17 402
— v Foster (unreported 4 July 1972) . . 202
— v Georgiou (1988) 4 BCC 322 . . . . . 402
— v Green and Green (1981) 3 Cr App R (S) 22 . . . . . . . . . . . . . . . . . . . . . 201
— v Russen & Ors (unreported 6 July 1984) . . . . . . . . . . . . . . . . . . . . . . 201
Russen & Ors; R v (unreported 6 July 1984) . . . . . . . . . . . . . . . . . . . . . . 201

**S**

Stanford Services Ltd & Ors, Re (1987) 3 BCC 326 . . . . . . . . . . . . . . . . . . . 412

**V**

VAB Plating Ltd, Re (ChD 11 April 1986) . . . . . . . . . . . . . . . . . . . . . . 202

**W**

Winkworth v Edward Baron Development Co Ltd & Ors [1987] 1 All ER 114; (1987) 3 BCC 4 . . . . . . . . . . . . 609

# Legislation Finding List

*All references are to paragraph numbers*


**Provision** — **Paragraph**

**Act of Sederunt (Company Directors Disqualification) 1986** . . . 107

**Building Societies Act 1986** . . . 1101
120 . . . 110
Sch. 18, para. 17(3) . . . 110

**Civil Liability (Contribution) Act 1978** . . 702

**Companies Act 1981** . . . 1103

**Companies Act 1985**
See generally . . . 101; 106; 107; 303; 801; 1105
117 . . . 803
173 . . . 804
295–302 . . . 301
295(2) . . . 302
296 . . . 301; 402
297 . . . 301; 403
298 . . . 301; 404
299 . . . 301
300 . . . 301; 302; 406; 410; 412; 1102
302 . . . 209
309 . . . 609
349(4) . . . 802
431–441 . . . 417
431 . . . 417
432(1) . . . 417
458 . . . 404; 501
447, 448 . . . 417
522 . . . 411
615 . . . 411
630 . . . 501; 503; 505
730(5) . . . 403
741(2) . . . 109
744 . . . 404
Sch. 12 . . . 301

**Companies (Disqualification Orders) Regulations 1986** . . . 107; 207

**Company Directors Disqualification Act 1986**
See generally . . . 101; 106; 107; 109; 210; 301; 303; 1101; 1105
1–5 . . . 107

**Provision** — **Paragraph**

1 . . . 901
1(1) . . . 201
1(3) . . . 208
2–5 . . . 204; 1103
2–10 . . . 202; 401
2 . . . 206; 301; 402; 404; 506; 1103
3 . . . 301; 403; 405; 414
3(1) . . . 1104
3(2), (3) . . . 403
3(3)(b) . . . 405
3(4) . . . 403
4 . . . 301; 404; 506
4(1)(a), (b) . . . 404
4(2) . . . 404
5 . . . 206; 301; 403; 405; 1104
5(2), (3) . . . 403
6–8 . . . 206
6–10 . . . 107; 110; 111; 1101
6 . . . 202; 204; 301; 404; 406; 407; 408; 410; 412; 415; 416; 419; 604; 1102
6(1) . . . 1002
6(1)(b) . . . 410; 413
6(2) . . . 407; 410; 419
6(3) . . . 413; 415
6(4) . . . 416
7 . . . 110
7(2) . . . 409
7(3) . . . 407; 408; 1002
7(4) . . . 408; 1002
8 . . . 204; 302; 304; 410; 412; 418; 419; 1102
9 . . . 410; 419
9(4) . . . 411
10 . . . 204; 302; 404; 416; 420; 506; 613
10(1) . . . 204
10(2) . . . 420
11 . . . 107; 108; 203; 209; 701; 702; 901
12 . . . 209
13–14 . . . 107
13 . . . 201
14, 14(1), (2) . . . 201

**Provision** **Paragraph**

**Company Directors Disqualification Act 1986**—*continued*
15 . . . 107; 111; 302; 701; 702; 703
15(1)(a), (b) . . . 702
15(2)–(5) . . . 702
16–18 . . . 107
16 . . . 206
16(2) . . . 204
17 . . . 903
18 . . . 207
19(c) . . . 111
20, 21(2) . . . 111
22(2) . . . 108
22(5) . . . 109
24 . . . 107
Sch. 1 . . . 107; 111; 407; 414; 419; 1101
Sch. 1, Pt. I . . . 410; 419
Sch. 1, para. 4 . . . 414
Sch. 1, Pt. II . . . 410
Sch. 1, paras 7, 8 . . . 411
Sch. 2, paras 1–4 . . . 1103
Sch. 2, para. 5 . . . 1104
Sch. 2, para. 6 . . . 1103
Sch. 2, paras 7, 8 . . . 1102
Sch. 3, paras 2–4 . . . 1105

**Company Securities (Insider Dealing) Act 1985**
1, 2, 4, 5, 105 . . . 417

**County Courts Act 1984**
Pt. VI . . . 209

**Criminal Justice Act 1987**
2 . . . 418

**Criminal Justice (Scotland) Act 1987** . . . 304
52 . . . 418
55(b) . . . 418

**Criminal Justice Act 1988**
145(b) . . . 418

**Financial Services Act 1986**
94 . . . 304; 417; 418
105 . . . 304; 418
177 . . . 304; 417; 418
198(2) . . . 304; 418

**Insolvency Act 1985**
See generally . . . 102; 103; 106; 110; 205; 303; 503; 1002; 1102; 1105
12–16 . . . 102; 107; 301; 1101
12, 13 . . . 302
15 . . . 1102
16 . . . 302
17 . . . 703
18 . . . 102; 107; 302; 1101

**Provision** **Paragraph**
101 . . . 411
Sch. 2 . . . 102; 107; 1101
Sch. 6, para. 1(3) . . . 302
Sch. 6, para. 6(1) . . . 505
Sch. 9 . . . 1102
Sch. 9, para. 4 . . . 1102

**Insolvency Act 1986**
See generally . . . 101; 106; 107; 108; 111; 403; 1101; 1105
1–7 . . . 404
4(1)(b) . . . 404
8 . . . 209; 404
76 . . . 804
86 . . . 606
98 . . . 410; 411
127 . . . 410; 411
129 . . . 606
212 . . . 110
213 . . . 107; 109; 110; 204; 404; 420; 501; 503; 505; 506
213(2) . . . 505
214–217 . . . 110
214 . . . 109; 204; 420; 503; 601; 602; 603; 605; 611; 612; 613; 615; 1101; 1102
214(2) . . . 1102
214(2)(b) . . . 604; 607
214(3) . . . 608
214(4) . . . 603; 607
214(4)(a) . . . 607
214(5) . . . 603; 607
214(7) . . . 604; 605
215 . . . 503; 505; 611
216 . . . 703
216(3) . . . 703
217 . . . 109
218(4), (5) . . . 417
Pt. V . . . 108; 111
220(1) . . . 108
238–240 . . . 410; 411
247 . . . 606
420 . . . 111
423 . . . 410
440, 441 . . . 107
Sch. 1 . . . 412
Sch. 11, paras 23–5 . . . 1105

**Insolvency Rules 1986**
r. 4.228–4.230 . . . 703

**Insolvent Companies (Disqualification of Unfit Directors) Proceedings Rules 1986** . 107

**Insolvent Companies (Disqualification of Unfit Directors) Proceedings Rules 1987** . 107; 206
r. 9 . . . 202

**Provision** **Paragraph**

**Insolvent Companies (Disqualification of Unfit Directors) Rules 1987**
r. 8(2) . . . . . . . . . . . . . . . . . . . . . . . . . 210

**Insolvent Companies (Reports on Conduct of Directors) Rules 1986** . . . . . . . . . . . 107

**Insolvent Companies (Reports on Conduct of Directors) No. 2 Rules 1986** . . 107; 1002

**Insolvent Companies (Reports on Conduct of Directors) (Scotland) Rules 1986**
59 . . . . . . . . . . . . . . . . . . . . . . . . . . . 107

**Provision** **Paragraph**

**Insolvent Companies (Reports on Conduct of Directors) (No. 2) (Scotland) Rules 1986**
140 . . . . . . . . . . . . . . . . . . . . . . . . . 107; 1002

**Insolvent Partnerships Order 1986** . 107; 111

**Insurance Companies Act 1982** . . . . . . . 402

**Law of Property Act 1925**
172 . . . . . . . . . . . . . . . . . . . . . . . . . . . . 411

# Index

*All references are to paragraph numbers*


Paragraph

A

**Accounts**
. duty to deliver, default ... 403

**Administration orders** ... 209; 407

**Administrative receiver** ... 407
. returns to Secretary of State ... 302

**Administrator**
. disqualification order ... 201

**Application for disqualification order** ... 204

**Assets**
. personal liability to contribute to . 302(3); 505

B

**Banks**
. liability ... 109

**Breach of disqualification order** ... 302(3); 701; 702

**Breach of duty** ... 301(3); 404

**Building societies**
. application of Insolvency Act 1986 ... 108; 110
. commencement dates of new legislation ... 1101
. re-use of prohibited names ... 704

C

**Cheques**
. company name wrongly stated, personal liability ... 802

**Companies**
. disqualification order against ... 201

**Companies Act 1985**
. disqualification orders, grounds for .. 301

Paragraph

**Company Directors Disqualification Act 1986** ... 106
. application and commencement ... 107
. application to bodies other than companies ... 108
. building societies, application to ... 110
. insolvent partnerships, winding up ... 111
. shadow directors, application to ... 109

**Company name**
. re-use of prohibited name ... 703
. . application for leave to use ... 705
. . building societies ... 704
. wrongly stated on cheques etc., personal liability ... 802

**Conviction of an indictable offence**
. disqualification order ... 402

**Cork Report** ... 103
. insolvency test ... 604
. personal liability, fraudulent trading . 502
. wrongful trading, anticipatory declarations ... 614

**Creditors**
. disqualification order application ... 204
. duties to ... 609

**Criminal offences**
. disqualification order, contravention . 201

**Customer prepayments**
. insolvent companies ... 412

D

**Debts**
. personal liability ... 702

**Default**
. filing documents etc. ... 301(2); 403

**Default orders** ... 405

**Definitions and meanings**
. fraudulent trading ... 404
. gone into insolvent liquidation ... 604

Paragraph

**Definitions and meanings**—*continued*
. insolvent company .............. 407
. management .................... 201
. officer ........................ 404
. officer in default ............. 403
. shadow directors ............... 109
. unfitness ...................... 410
. unregistered company ........... 108
. wrongful trading ............... 603

**Department of Trade and Industry**
. Director Disqualification Unit ...... 205
. inspectors' reports ............. 304

**Director Disqualification Unit** ........ 205

**Directors**
. creditors, duties to ............ 609
. default .................. 301; 403
. definition ..................... 605
. disqualification—see Disqualification; Disqualification orders
. personal liability—see Personal liability

**Disqualification**
. Companies Act 1985, under ....... 301
. consolidating legislation ....... 303
. Financial Services Act 1986 ...... 304
. Insolvency Act 1985 changes ...... 302
. orders—see Disqualification orders
. undischarged bankrupt ........... 209

**Disqualification orders**
. administration .................. 205
. application for ................. 204
. breach, personal liability ...... 701; 702
. contravention ............... 201; 302
. duration ....................... 202
. enforcement .................... 205
. fraudulent trading .......... 402; 506
. grounds for .................... 401
. . breach of duty revealed in winding-up ............... 404
. . Companies Act 1985 ........... 301
. . conviction of an indictable offence . 402
. . fraud revealed in winding-up ..... 404
. . fraudulent trading revealed in winding-up ............... 404
. . persistent breaches of companies legislation ............... 403
. insolvent companies ............. 406
. . conduct in relation to other companies ................ 413
. . definition ................... 407
. . judicial decisions on question of unfitness ................. 412
. . liquidator's report on directors' conduct .................. 408

Paragraph

. . preference .................. 411
. . time-limit .................. 409
. . transactions at an undervalue ..... 411
. . unfitness, meaning ......... 410; 414
. . unsecured creditors ........... 411
. investigations
. . Secretarey of State's application ... 418; 419
. . statutory powers ............. 417
. leave of court to act during currency of order ..................... 203
. . conditions .................. 905
. . court to which application is made . 903
. . procedure ................... 904
. . statutory provisions ............ 901
. . time and mode of application ..... 902
. more than one ................. 208
. nature and effect ............... 201
. non-cumulative ............. 208; 302
. register of .................... 207
. summary conviction under companies legislation ................ 405
. time limits .............. 202; 301; 405
. variation ...................... 210
. wrongful trading ........... 420; 613

**Documents**
. duty to deliver, default .......... 403
. failure to keep ................ 412

F

**Former directors** ................ 109
. insolvent companies ............. 415
. wrongful trading ............ 605; 610

**Fraud**
. disqualification order ....... 301(3); 404

**Fraudulent trading**—see also **Wrongful trading**
. disqualification order ...... 404; 420; 506
. insolvent partnerships ........... 507
. law in force .................... 504
. personal liability ............... 501
. . Cork Committee .............. 502
. . remedies and procedure ......... 505

I

**Indictable offences**
. disqualification order ....... 301(1); 402

**Insolvency Act 1985**
. Cork Report .................... 103
. director disqualification ......... 302

Paragraph

**Insolvency Act 1985**—*continued*
. Insolvency Bill . . . . . . . . . . . . . . . . . 105
. reforms introduced . . . . . . . . . . . . . . 102
. White Paper of 1984 . . . . . . . . . . . . . 104

**Insolvency Act 1986** . . . . . . . . . . . . . . . 106
. application and commencement . . . . . 107
. application to bodies other than companies . . . . . . . . . . . . . . . . . 108
. building society directors . . . . . . . . . . 110
. insolvent partnerships, winding up . . . 111
. shadow directors, application to . . . . 109

**Insolvency practitioner**
. qualifications . . . . . . . . . . . . . . . . . . 1001
. report on conduct of directors of insolvent company . . . . . . . . . . 1002

**Insolvent companies**
. definition . . . . . . . . . . . . . . . . . . . . 407
. disqualification orders . . . . . . . . . . . . 406
. . duration of order . . . . . . . . . . . . . . 416
. insolvency practitioner's report on conduct of directors . . . . . . . . . 1002
. liquidator's report on directors' conduct . . . . . . . . . . . . . . . . . . 408
. time-limit for disqualification application . . . . . . . . . . . . . . . . . 409
. unfitness
. . conduct in relation to other companies . . . . . . . . . . . . . . . . . 413
. . implications of new definition . . . . . 414
. . judicial decisions . . . . . . . . . . . . . . 412
. . meaning . . . . . . . . . . . . . . . . . . . . 410
. . shadow directors and former directors . . . . . . . . . . . . . . . . . 415

**Insolvent partnerships**
. fraudulent trading . . . . . . . . . . . . . . . 507
. winding-up . . . . . . . . . . . . . . . . . . . . 111

**Investigations**
. disqualification following . . . . . . . . 302(2)
. statutory powers . . . . . . . . . . . . . . . . 417
. unfitness of directors . . . . . . . . . . . . . 206

L

**Liability**—see **Personal liability**

**Limited liability**
. loss of protection of . . . . . . . . . . . . . 801

**Liquidators**
. disqualification order
. . application for . . . . . . . . . . . . . . . . 204
. . prohibition from acting as . . . . . . . 201
. report on directors' conduct . . . . . . . 408

Paragraph

M

**Managers**
. disqualification order . . . . . . . . . . . . . 201

**Members**
. disqualification order application . . . . 204

O

**Official Receiver**
. disqualification order application . . . . 204

P

**Partnerships**
. insolvent
. . fraudulent trading . . . . . . . . . . . . . 507
. . winding-up . . . . . . . . . . . . . . . . . . 111

**Personal liability**
. breach of disqualification order . 701; 702
. cheques etc., company name wrongly stated . . . . . . . . . . . . . . . . . . . . . 802
. Companies Act 1985, under . . . . . . . 801
. fraudulent trading . . . . . . . . . . . . . . . 501
. . Cork Committee . . . . . . . . . . . . . . 502
. . law in force . . . . . . . . . . . . . . . . . . 504
. . remedies and procedure . . . . . . . . . 505
. loss of limited liability protection . . . . 801
. public company commencing business prematurely . . . . . . . . . . . . . . . 803
. re-use of prohibited company name . . 703
. . application for leave to use . . . . . . 705
. . building societies . . . . . . . . . . . . . 704
. shares purchased or redeemed out of capital . . . . . . . . . . . . . . . . . . . . 804
. wrongful trading
. . before commencement of winding-up . . . . . . . . . . . . . . . . . 606
. . concept of . . . . . . . . . . . . . . . . . . . 601
. . exoneration . . . . . . . . . . . . . . . . . . 608
. . former director . . . . . . . . . . . . . . . 605
. . gone into insolvent liquidation, meaning . . . . . . . . . . . . . . . . . . 604
. . knowledge, skill and experience . . . 607
. . marginal note irrelevant . . . . . . . . . 602
. . new law, implications . . . . . . . . . . . 609
. . payments, application . . . . . . . . . . 612
. . practical consequences . . . . . . . . . . 610
. . procedure . . . . . . . . . . . . . . . . . . . 611
. . shadow director . . . . . . . . . . . . . . . 605
. . statutory definition . . . . . . . . . . . . 603

**Preference** . . . . . . . . . . . . . . . . . . . . . 411

Paragraph

**Prohibited company name**—see **Company name**

**Public company**
. commencing business prematurely, personal liability . . . . . . . . . . . . . 803

R

**Receivers**
. disqualification order . . . . . . . . . . . . . 201

**Register of disqualification orders** . . . . . 207

**Remuneration**
. drawing excessive . . . . . . . . . . . . . . . 412

**Returns**
. duty to make, default . . . . . . . . . . . . 403
. failure to file . . . . . . . . . . . . . . . . . . . 412
. office-holders of insolvent companies . 408

S

**Salaries**
. paying when company insolvent . . . . . 412

**Secretary of State**
. disqualification order application . . . . 204
. insolvent companies, liquidator's report . . . . . . . . . . . . . . . . . . . 408
. investigations, appointment of inspectors . . . . . . . . . . . . . . . . 417
. returns to . . . . . . . . . . . . . . . . . . . . 302

**Shadow directors**
. insolvent companies . . . . . . . . . . . . . 415
. liability . . . . . . . . . . . . . . . . . . . . . . . 109
. wrongful trading . . . . . . . . . . . . . . . . 605

**Shares**
. purchased or redeemed out of capital, personal liability . . . . . . . . . . . . . 804

**Statement of affairs**
. failure to submit . . . . . . . . . . . . . . . . 412

**Summary conviction** . . . . . . . . . 301(5); 405

T

**Time limits for disqualification** . . . . . . . . 202; 405; 409; 416

**Trading**
. insolvent company, by . . . . . . . . . . . . 412

**Transactions at undervalue** . . . . . . . . . . 411

**Transitional provisions**
. commencement dates of new legislation . . . . . . . . . . . . . . . . 1101
. disqualification provisions, commencement dates . . . . 1101; 1103
. events before 28 April 1986 . . . . . . . 1102
. offences and default orders before 1 June 1977 . . . . . . . . . . . . . . . . 1104
. subordinate legislation . . . . . . . . . . 1105
. wrongful trading provisions, commencement dates . . . . . . . . 1101

U

**Undervalue**
. transactions at . . . . . . . . . . . . . . . . . . 411

**Undischarged bankrupt** . . . . . . . . . . . . . 108
. disqualification, acting as director or liquidator . . . . . . . . . . . . . . . . . . 209
. leave to act by court . . . . . . . . . . . . . 203

**Unfitness**
. definition . . . . . . . . . . . . . . . . . . . . . 410
. disqualification order sought . . . . . . . 206
. . grounds . . . . . . . . . . . . . . . . . . . . 302
. insolvent companies . . . . . . . . . . . . . 406
. judicial decisions . . . . . . . . . . . . . . . . 412

**Unregistered company**
. application of Insolvency Act 1986 . . . 108

**Unsecured creditors** . . . . . . . . . . . . . . . 411

W

**Winding-up**
. breach of duty . . . . . . . . . . . . . . . . . . 404
. fraud . . . . . . . . . . . . . . . . . . . . . . . . 404
. fraudulent trading . . . . . . . . . . . . . . . 404
. insolvent partnerships . . . . . . . . . . . . 111
. personal liability, wrongful trading . . 606

**Wrongful trading**—see also **Fraudulent trading**
. anticipatory declarations . . . . . . . . . . 614
. disqualification order . . . . . . . . . 420; 613
. . grounds . . . . . . . . . . . . . . . . . . . . 302
. judicial ruling . . . . . . . . . . . . . . . . . . 615
. new law . . . . . . . . . . . . . . . . . . . . . . 503
. personal liability
. . before commencement of winding-up . . . . . . . . . . . . . . . . 606
. . concept of wrongful trading . . . . . . 601
. . exoneration . . . . . . . . . . . . . . . . . . 608
. . former director . . . . . . . . . . . . . . . 605
. . gone into insolvent liquidation, meaning . . . . . . . . . . . . . . . . . . 604
. . knowledge, skill and experience . . . 607
. . marginal note irrelevant . . . . . . . . . 602

Paragraph

**Wrongful trading**—*continued*
. . new law, implications . . . . . . . . . . . 609
. . payments, application . . . . . . . . . . 612
. . practical consequences . . . . . . . . . . 610

Paragraph

. . procedure . . . . . . . . . . . . . . . . . . . 611
. . shadow director . . . . . . . . . . . . . . . 605
. . statutory definition . . . . . . . . . . . . 603